THIS BOOK BELONGS TO:

_____

Emmanuel

ORIGINAL ART AND TEXT BY

RUTH CHOU SIMONS

HARVEST HOUSE PUBLISHERS
EUGENE, OREGON

Published in association with William K. Jensen Literary Agency, 119 Bampton Court, Eugene, OR 97404

Original artwork by Ruth Chou Simons; design work by Sarah Alexander

Cover and interior design by Janelle Coury

For bulk, special sales, or ministry purchases, please call 1-800-547-8979.
Email: Customerservice@hhpbooks.com

Copyright © 2022 by Ruth Chou Simons
Published by Harvest House Publishers
Eugene, Oregon 97408
www.harvesthousepublishers.com

ISBN 978-0-7369-8496-6 (hardcover)
ISBN 978-0-7369-8497-3 (eBook)

Library of Congress Cataloging-in-Publication Data is on file at the Library of Congress, Washington, DC

Printed in China

22 23 24 25 26 27 28 29 30 / RRD / 10 9 8 7 6 5 4 3 2 1

To the ones who believe it's possible
to know God with us all year long...
long after the twinkle lights are tucked away.
You are my people.
This one's for you and yours.

Contents

A Word from Ruth... 7

A Note About the Book Title................................. 9

WEEK ONE Our Posture.................................... 11

DAY *1* From Expectations to Expectant 17

DAY *2* From Worried to Worshipful 27

DAY *3* From Lacking to Generous 35

DAY *4* From Isolated to Invited 43

DAY *5* From Stressed to Grateful 51

DAY *6* From Jealous to Joyful 59

WEEK TWO God's Promise................................ 67

DAY *7* A Relationship 73

DAY *8* A Wonderful Savior 81

DAY *9* A Merciful God 89

DAY *10* A Coming Messiah 97

DAY 11   A Redeemer 105

DAY 12   A Transformed Life 113

WEEK THREE   Our Response 121

DAY 13   Awe + Wonder 127

DAY 14   Faith 135

DAY 15   Repentance 143

DAY 16   Thanksgiving 151

DAY 17   Love 159

DAY 18   Worship 167

WEEK FOUR   Our Messiah 175

DAY 19   Wonderful Counselor 179

DAY 20   Mighty God 187

DAY 21   Everlasting Father 195

DAY 22   Prince of Peace 203

DAY 23   Lord of Lords 211

DAY 24   Immanuel 219

DAY 25   Christmas Day 227

Notes 233

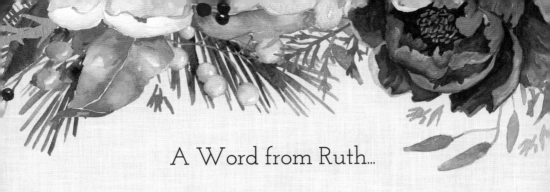

A Word from Ruth...

Friend,

I pray you've picked up this book because you long for something richer and more satisfying than good food, dear friends, and fulfilled wish lists this Christmas season. My hope is that, like me, you want to discover something in the Advent season that will outlast the month of December. What if we allow the truths of "God with us" to shape everything we do all year long? What if we let the Christmas story fill our hearts so that it changes the way we celebrate the season and live the rest of the year? Maybe the weariness we feel during this time every year is a result of expectations that lean too much on the things of the season and not enough on Christ. We must prepare Him room.

My hope is this book will meet you (and your family and friends) right where you are. I pray its pages will draw you in with beauty and truth, and that its message will remind you that we were created to know much more than the bustle, or even the magic, of Christmas. We were made to know Christ.

Ruth

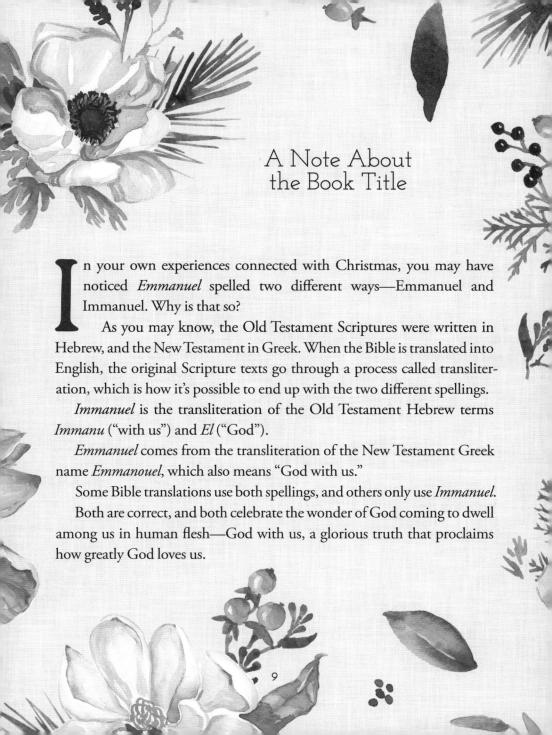

A Note About the Book Title

In your own experiences connected with Christmas, you may have noticed *Emmanuel* spelled two different ways—Emmanuel and Immanuel. Why is that so?

As you may know, the Old Testament Scriptures were written in Hebrew, and the New Testament in Greek. When the Bible is translated into English, the original Scripture texts go through a process called transliteration, which is how it's possible to end up with the two different spellings.

Immanuel is the transliteration of the Old Testament Hebrew terms *Immanu* ("with us") and *El* ("God").

Emmanuel comes from the transliteration of the New Testament Greek name *Emmanouel*, which also means "God with us."

Some Bible translations use both spellings, and others only use *Immanuel*.

Both are correct, and both celebrate the wonder of God coming to dwell among us in human flesh—God with us, a glorious truth that proclaims how greatly God loves us.

The angel said to her, "Do not be afraid, Mary, for you have found favor with God. And behold, you will conceive in your womb and bear a son, and you shall call his name Jesus. He will be great and will be called the Son of the Most High..."

And Mary said to the angel, "How will this be, since I am a virgin?"

And the angel answered her, "The Holy Spirit will come upon you, and the power of the Most High will overshadow you; therefore the child to be born will be called holy—the Son of God..." And Mary said, "Behold, I am the servant of the Lord; let it be to me according to your word."

Luke 1:30-38

WEEK ONE

Our posture

WEEK ONE

Our posture

From right where you are—don't move: Pay attention to your posture in this moment, from the top of your head to the tips of your toes. Take note of how you are sitting, standing, or how your neck and shoulders feel. What is your current posture? Are you leaning over your kitchen counter? Reclined at the dinner table? Lying down? Tense? Feeling rushed or relaxed? Whether we realize it or not, we operate out of the posture of our hearts, and most often, that posture reveals itself in subtle and not-so-subtle ways in our physical posture as well.

If you look around any coffee shop, you'll notice many of the peppermint-mocha-drinking customers hunched over their laptops or looking down at their cell phones. Even in a laid-back environment like a coffee shop, people are busy and hustling. We spend the majority of our days poring over the devices of our busy lives, and sometimes we catch ourselves bowing our hearts before the flashing images across our screens as well. And we wonder why we are so worn out and tense. Posture matters. But whether we sit up properly or use an ergonomic chair, the posture—or the position and bent—of our hearts matters even more.

POSTURE DETERMINES OUR APPROACH
AND TRAJECTORY ON ANY JOURNEY.

When given God's plan for her role in the incarnation of Christ, Mary said, "Behold, I am the servant of the Lord; let it be to me according to your word." Her heart posture readied her for a plan she didn't even fully understand; she simply trusted God, and that trust made room for all His plans to unfold in and through her.

Posture determines our approach and trajectory on any journey. It's the unseen rudder that directs the way we welcome any circumstance...and any season.

And so, as we begin this Advent journey, we begin with our posture, because how we enter this season affects how we will receive this season. Let's realign ourselves with the true hope of Christmas, and reposition ourselves with a heart posture that is ready to receive all that is intended for us in this Advent season.

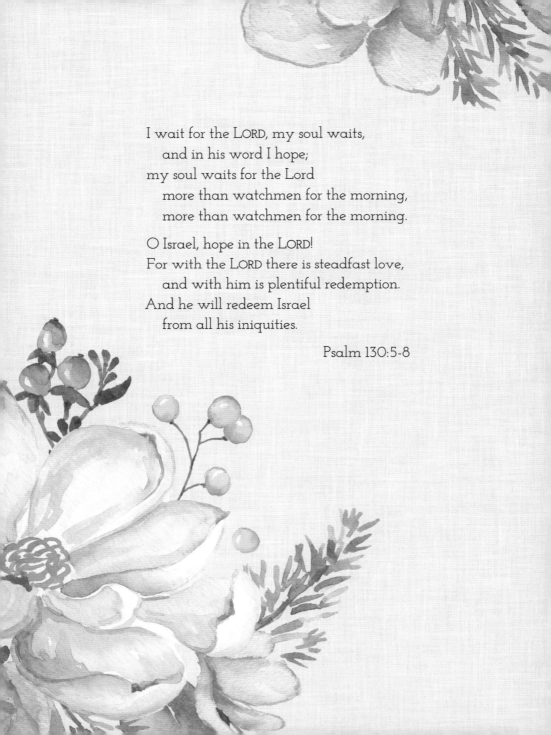

I wait for the LORD, my soul waits,
    and in his word I hope;
my soul waits for the Lord
    more than watchmen for the morning,
    more than watchmen for the morning.

O Israel, hope in the LORD!
For with the LORD there is steadfast love,
    and with him is plentiful redemption.
And he will redeem Israel
    from all his iniquities.

Psalm 130:5-8

Day 1

From Expectations to Expectant

We've all been there: A long-awaited family vacation, a special event, an important milestone birthday…a highly anticipated celebration. And then, out of the blue, something totally unexpected happens and ruins everything (at least from our human perspective). Can you think of the last time a special occasion or holiday season let you down? Our human expectations are prone to disappointment. We get our hearts wrapped around things we think we need or circumstances we desire, and when those things (or expectations) don't satisfy as we hope, we're left deflated and sometimes even jaded, numb, or unengaged.

Many of us lack the eager anticipation we once knew in our youth when it comes to Christmastime. Ask yourself: Does the first sign of Christmas decor stir your heart up with giddiness, or does the mere sight of pre-lit Christmas trees and gift wrap cause you anxiety? The ambience set by merchandisers is meant to ignite our excitement and preparation for a festive season, but for so many of us, the joyous expectancy of a fun-filled holiday is overshadowed by unrealistic expectations and impossible standards. We replace expectancy with expectations.

Christmas is the celebration of the birth of Christ, but the Israelites, who anticipated the promise of a Messiah, waited hundreds of years for this promise to be fulfilled. Along the way, God revealed His purposes and plans little by little, and sometimes the people waited eagerly, and other times, impatiently. Do you remember when the Israelites crafted a golden calf because they grew impatient and took matters into their own hands?

How one waits affects how he or she follows God's lead, or doesn't. Did you know your heart posture, which can be hidden, affects so much that is evident in your everyday life?

The stories we tell ourselves about any season—especially the Christmas season—shape how we feel and act in response. If you expect Christmastime to make you feel good about your family relationships, you will be disappointed. If you expect your spouse to read your mind about what makes a holiday season special, you will be disappointed. If you expect gifts from others to make you feel loved and remembered, you will be disappointed. You see, what we believe we are waiting for in this season affects our posture, and that, in turn, determines the difference between whether we are overjoyed or overwhelmed.

The Psalms are such beautiful reflections of the psalmist's heart posture in various seasons and circumstances. In Psalm 130, we see the psalmist sing a song of hope—from a place of distress and need, he declares what is true about God's forgiveness, faithfulness, and steadfast love. The psalmist acknowledges that he has an audience with God because God graciously forgives (verse 3). He knows he's been given more than he deserves, and he now waits for his loving God to faithfully provide again. He doesn't question whether God hears his need. Rather, he is expectant, knowing that God keeps His promises. It's this very confidence and expectancy in a good and

Expectant

I WAIT FOR THE LORD,
MY SOUL WAITS...

He is faithful

faithful God that led Corrie ten Boom to anticipate the same of her heavenly Father:

> When Jesus takes your hand, He keeps you tight. When Jesus keeps you tight, He leads you through your whole life. When Jesus leads you through your whole life, He brings you safely home.[1]

Christmas is a homecoming—one where the broken of humanity are given access to the home they were meant for in Christ. Our only means of coming home to Jesus is to welcome and prepare Him room right where we are.

WHEN WE TURN FROM EXPECTATIONS TO BEING EXPECTANT, WE WILL NEVER BE DISAPPOINTED BECAUSE GOD NEVER DISAPPOINTS.

Expectations leave us weary and discontent, believing we deserve more or better. They always leave us unfulfilled and doubtful about whether God is for our good. But expectancy is anticipation mingled with joy. It's believing God is who He says He is while waiting patiently for His good to be revealed, however He chooses to reveal it. Expectancy remembers what is already more than one deserves; expectation demands more. When we come to the Christmas season with an expectant posture, we're led in hope—like the wise men led by the star. Expectancy sets our sights on God's promises rather than the empty pursuit of all that cannot truly satisfy in this season. When we turn from expectations to being expectant, we will never be disappointed because God never disappoints. What He promises, He will do.

PONDER

Are you more consumed with expectations in this
season, or with anticipation for how God has fulfilled—
and will continue to fulfill—His promises?

PRAISE

Come, Thou Long-Expected Jesus

PRAY

Dear Father, we praise You for all You have done and
have yet to do. Help us to long for You alone rather than
the expectations and desires that do not satisfy. Realign
our hearts according to Your Word, that we might have a
heart posture ready to receive Your provisions. And when
we're tempted to bend toward our earthly desires and
ways of thinking, teach us to recount Your faithfulness
and remember that You are God. While we wait for Your
purpose to be revealed, while we look to Your Word, soften
our hearts to trust in You instead of ourselves. Amen.

WHEN JESUS TAKES YOUR HAND, HE
KEEPS YOU TIGHT. WHEN JESUS KEEPS
YOU TIGHT, HE LEADS YOU THROUGH
YOUR WHOLE LIFE. WHEN JESUS
LEADS YOU THROUGH YOUR WHOLE
LIFE, HE BRINGS YOU SAFELY HOME.

CORRIE TEN BOOM

Now as they went on their way, Jesus entered a village. And a woman named Martha welcomed him into her house. And she had a sister called Mary, who sat at the Lord's feet and listened to his teaching. But Martha was distracted with much serving. And she went up to him and said, "Lord, do you not care that my sister has left me to serve alone? Tell her then to help me." But the Lord answered her, "Martha, Martha, you are anxious and troubled about many things, but one thing is necessary. Mary has chosen the good portion, which will not be taken away from her."

Luke 10:38-42

Day 2

From Worried to Worshipful

The story of Mary and Martha is so relatable for many of us during the Christmas season. Maybe we can recall a time we muttered under our breath while alone in the kitchen preparing for a big meal. Or perhaps a time we've been given chores to do while our sibling is taking it easy on the couch. *Clean up your own mess!* we fuss in our minds. Or maybe we've found ourselves fretting about the condition of our dishes or decor, wishing we could've completely remodeled before the entire family descended in our home for the holidays. (Do we have an amen from some of the moms in the room?) You see, we can all relate to Martha every day, but especially during the holidays. For a people who proclaim that "Jesus is the reason for the season" or that Christ is the most important part of Christmas, we sure do worry about a lot of other things during this season.

What if I don't have enough food? Why can't my dishes be prettier? What if the cousins get in a fight? How can I host when I'm so worn out? What if no one pitches in?

The questions and concerns themselves are not wrong to consider, but as was the case when Mary and Martha hosted Jesus in their home, they aren't the most important things.

When Martha asks Jesus to tell her sister Mary to help her in the kitchen, Jesus doesn't scold Martha for being responsible, hard-working, or eager to serve. He doesn't tell her to *just relax* and isn't ambivalent about hospitality. Instead, Jesus is compassionate. He lets her know He *sees her.* He sees Martha's anxious thoughts...her worry, her frustration, even her pouting. He sees how she wants to do the right thing, but then becomes bitter in the process. Jesus doesn't downplay service and work in His response to Martha; He elevates surrender and worship.

Mary, on the other hand, worships at Jesus' feet. She fixes her eyes on Him, listens eagerly, and finds rest with Him. This reflects the posture of her heart. And it is that heart posture that Jesus calls "the good portion."

WORSHIP BEGINS WHEN WE BOW OUR HEARTS
BEFORE JESUS AND TRUST HIM FOR ALL
THAT WE CAN'T FIX ON OUR OWN...WHICH,
AS IT TURNS OUT, IS *EVERYTHING.*

We don't need a sanctuary or a symphony orchestra to worship. No stained glass is required. No choirs or praise bands must lead us in song. We don't even need a candlelit service to set the mood. Worship begins when we bow our hearts before Jesus and trust Him for all that we can't fix on our own...which, as it turns out, is *everything.*

A.W. Tozer said, "We are called to an everlasting preoccupation with God."[2] That means if a mind is filled with worry, it will be too preoccupied to focus on worship. But, alternatively, a mind consumed with worship will not have the capacity for worry; it will be too preoccupied with the goodness of God. You see, the antidote to a worried heart is a worshipful one.

Worshipful

MARY HAS CHOSEN THE
GOOD PORTION...

the good portion

Distracted, anxious, troubled, feeling bitter that we are doing all the work, our hosting and gift-giving preparations can quickly steal our joy and become our focus during the Advent season. When we fret over unforeseen circumstances and fuss over impressing others, we miss what Jesus calls "the one thing" that's necessary—a posture of worship. Jesus came that we might know His presence, not impress anyone with our own.

So while there is a place for plans, lists, and preparation, let us not mistake the busyness of *doing* in this season for the fruitfulness of *worship*. Don't let the worry over *how* to celebrate the birth of Christ at Christmas eclipse the wonder of actually *worshipping* Jesus Christ, the long-awaited Messiah.

He sees you—right in the midst of all your cares and concerns. He sees how you're torn, like Martha, between service and surrender, worry and worship. And He invites you to lay down the fretting and choose "the good portion"— to choose worship. After all, it's the very invitation He came to earth to give.

PONDER

What do you tend to worry about during the Christmas season?
How does worshipping Jesus alone change your heart posture?

PRAISE

What Child Is This?

PRAY

Heavenly Father, in this season, help us to not confuse
doing with *worship*. Because You so loved us, help us to
love You in return and serve out of an overflow of that love.
And when we feel worried and overwhelmed, help us to
choose what is first and best—to sit at Your feet. Refresh us
by Your Spirit and cause us to serve with gladness. Amen.

OH COME, LET US WORSHIP
AND BOW DOWN;
LET US KNEEL BEFORE
THE LORD, OUR MAKER!

PSALM 95:6

One of the Pharisees asked him to eat with him, and he went into the Pharisee's house and reclined at table. And behold, a woman of the city, who was a sinner, when she learned that he was reclining at table in the Pharisee's house, brought an alabaster flask of ointment, and standing behind him at his feet, weeping, she began to wet his feet with her tears and wiped them with the hair of her head and kissed his feet and anointed them with the ointment.

Luke 7:36-38

Day 3

From Lacking to Generous

I t's not hard to feel as if the blessings of the Christmas season are intertwined with financial means and abundance. For those of us in the Western world, so much of the anticipation and joy seems directly related to the parties we throw, the gifts we give, or the places we go. Whether we realize it or not, we can easily buy into the lie that Christmas abundance is measured in fun memories, lots of friends, and all the things our hearts desire wrapped under the tree. Clearly, we're missing Jesus' definition and idea of abundance, which is all about a generous heart.

The story of the sinful woman who anointed Jesus' feet with oil is a picture of unlikely abundance. In Jesus' day, when guests entered a home, washing their feet was a customary sign of respect, as dirty feet were to be expected in ancient times. Simon, a Pharisee who would've been a religiously and financially privileged member of society, did not offer to wash Jesus' feet, but the sinful woman—one with a shameful reputation—generously anointed His feet with her tears and the entire contents of a flask of perfumed oil, worth at least a year's wages in that day. Jesus didn't draw attention to the cost of the oil spilled over His feet; He simply called attention to the posture of her heart.

WE LACK NOTHING WHEN JESUS IS
OUR GREATEST TREASURE.

For the sinful woman, Jesus was worth it all. Awareness of her own great sin made her even more aware of the forgiveness of a *greater* Savior. What surely felt extravagant and wasteful to onlookers was an overflow of the generosity in her own heart of love toward Jesus. This woman—who could've considered herself unworthy, lacking, and not enough in the eyes of others—found welcome, forgiveness, and blessing from Jesus.

We don't need to come into this season *lacking*. Like the woman who poured all she had upon the feet of Jesus, we lack nothing when Jesus is our greatest treasure.

How is Jesus our greatest treasure? Ephesians 1:3 says that God the Father "has blessed us in Christ with every spiritual blessing in the heavenly places." That means that Jesus fulfills every longing of our hearts. Peace? Victory? Strength? Joy? Hope eternal? A clean conscience? The Bible tells us that Jesus is the one who makes all these and more not just possible, but securely ours, when we are in Christ.

While the world clamors for material abundance, we who know Jesus have nothing to lose in our generous giving, and nothing to gain that is more valuable than our redemption in Christ. We can take our eyes off worldly abundance and fix them on Jesus. We can stop counting up all that we think we lack and start living into all that we've been given on account of Christ. When we remember where our true treasure comes from, our posture changes from *not enough* to *more than we deserve*.

generous
...GO IN PEACE.

More than we deserve

PONDER

What is your valuable "alabaster flask of ointment," and in what ways can you use it to bless and glorify Christ?

PRAISE

God Rest Ye Merry Gentlemen

PRAY

Dear Father, You are good and so very generous with us. Though we so often misjudge our provisions and blessings, You are patient with us. Teach us to rightly assess the gravity of our sin that we might respond to Your gift of grace and mercy as You deserve—with awe, wonder, and total surrender. May we, on account of your abundant love for us, take that which is most valuable to us and give it back to you—generously. Amen.

NO MAN EVER
ERRS ON THE
SIDE OF GIVING
TOO MUCH
HONOR TO GOD
THE SON.

J.C. RYLE

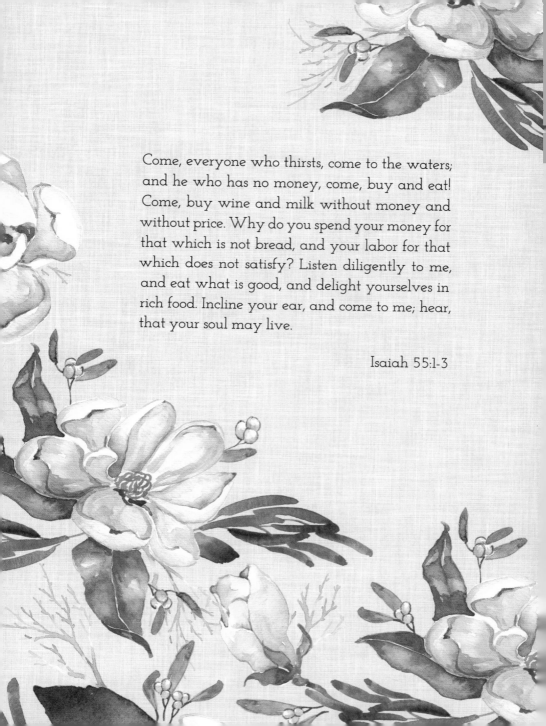

Come, everyone who thirsts, come to the waters; and he who has no money, come, buy and eat! Come, buy wine and milk without money and without price. Why do you spend your money for that which is not bread, and your labor for that which does not satisfy? Listen diligently to me, and eat what is good, and delight yourselves in rich food. Incline your ear, and come to me; hear, that your soul may live.

Isaiah 55:1-3

Day 4

From Isolated to Invited

For one reason or another, there are times in life when we feel very, very alone. Maybe unexpected life circumstances have isolated you. Maybe you didn't receive an invitation to a gathering of colleagues or friends. Maybe you feel distant or estranged from family this Christmas season, and every commercial about *coming home* and family reunions stings and deepens the festering hurt in your life.

Or maybe the feeling of loneliness goes deeper than that, and you struggle to feel like you belong...anywhere. Some of us feel as though we've been abandoned, betrayed, left out, overlooked, and, truth be told, we all know times we have. The hunger we feel for fellowship, for true friendship, for a place to belong...is meant to be filled and satisfied.

But there's no one! I feel so alone! we're tempted to think.

GOD MADE US TO HUNGER AND THIRST FOR HIM; WE SHOULDN'T BE SURPRISED WHEN NOTHING ELSE SATISFIES.

We may find this hard to believe, but it's in the very desperation of solitude in life's lonely moments that we come to realize our need for a good and soul-satisfying Savior. Would we recognize our need for Him otherwise? God made us to hunger and thirst for Him; we shouldn't be surprised when nothing else satisfies. The psalmist sets a good example for us on how to turn the posture of our hearts from yearning to hoping in God. He preaches truth to himself and tells his soul what to do:

> As a deer pants for flowing streams, so pants my soul for you, O God. My soul thirsts for God, for the living God...Why are you cast down, O my soul, and why are you in turmoil within me? Hope in God; for I shall again praise him, my salvation and my God (Psalm 42:1-2, 11).

The psalmist knew where he had to direct his longing heart, and we can follow his lead. We can turn from our isolation to the invitation and welcome of our God. He who says, "Come, everyone who thirsts" in Isaiah 55:1 is the same who spoke through Jesus, "Come to me, all you who are weary and burdened, and I will give you rest" (Matthew 11:28 NIV).

Our loneliness and isolation are often reminders that we aren't meant to bear our burdens alone. While friendships and invitations are joys in this life, the invitation from Jesus to find everything we need in Him is joy everlasting.

So for all of us who sometimes struggle with feelings of loss and loneliness rather than warmth and celebration in the Christmas season, we are not alone. As Christ-followers, we need not hope in party invitations or chaos-free family gatherings; we have the ultimate welcome in the kingdom of God. His welcome is for you and His welcome is for me. Jesus comforts, cares, and provides for those who long for all things made new and a

Invited

COME, EVERYONE
WHO THIRSTS...

delight in Him

fellowship that never ends. And as it turns out, when you receive His invitation, He'll never let you go.

> The LORD himself goes before you and will be with you;
> he will never leave you nor forsake you.
> Do not be afraid; do not be discouraged
> (Deuteronomy 31:8 NIV).

PONDER

How have you experienced the comfort and care of Jesus?

PRAISE

I Wonder as I Wander

PRAY

Father, we thank You that You promise to never leave us nor forsake us. Your presence is not a feeling, but true companionship in Christ. When we feel alone, afraid, or forgotten, remind us that we are held by the promise of Your Word: We are never alone. As vessels of the living God, lead us to be conduits of comfort, grace, and companionship to others who feel alone...that we might share our belonging in Jesus with a lonely world. Amen.

AS A DEER
PANTS FOR
FLOWING
STREAMS, SO
PANTS MY SOUL
FOR YOU, O GOD.

PSALM 42:1

Rejoice in the Lord always; again I will say, rejoice. Let your reasonableness be known to everyone. The Lord is at hand; do not be anxious about anything, but in everything by prayer and supplication with thanksgiving let your requests be made known to God. And the peace of God, which surpasses all understanding, will guard your hearts and your minds in Christ Jesus.

Philippians 4:4-7

Day 5

From Stressed to Grateful

ometimes our cluttered homes reflect our cluttered hearts. You know how it is to rifle through a messy drawer, unable to find what you're looking for. Or when you must move piles and stacks of mail and papers on a counter just to have enough surface to work on. And then there's the kind of clutter that builds up over days, months, and years—the kind that overwhelms and engulfs you with its relentless oppression, as if to taunt and accuse: *You're such a mess. You're so disorganized. No one likes you. You'll always be stressed, scatterbrained, and overwhelmed.*

We've all known times when these lies, or worse, have looped endlessly in our minds. And we're tempted to believe them as we look around at our homes and daily routines. Do you know that stress isn't just an adult issue? No age or season of life is exempt when it comes to the feeling of pressure and clutter in our minds and hearts. In one way or another, we all know what it means to live stressed-out lives. Kids running from soccer games to ballet classes to music lessons. Teens overwhelmed by college applications and the pressure to be better than their peers. Moms and dads trying to make everyone happy and keep everything afloat. Stress has become so common in our everyday lives that we don't even attempt to hide its repercussions or effects. "I'm so stressed!" we declare weekly...and sometimes daily.

We diagnose the problem and believe our solution is a cleaner bedroom (that could help!), more smartphone apps to keep our tasks in order, better storage containers, a long vacation to unwind, or more time to untangle the mess. All those things can be helpful, but the presence of stress in our lives has more to do with our hearts than our circumstances (even if a change in circumstances will help reframe our hearts!). According to the Bible, our stress and anxiety are the result of trying to fix our problems on our own when, instead, we are called to pray with a grateful heart.

The Christmas season is often hijacked by the stress we allow to direct the posture of our hearts. Sure, we can simplify by buying less kitschy decor, or by changing up our family's gift-buying routine, and such efforts to simplify may very well make a difference. But don't be fooled; if peace is what we seek, we will find its true source only in Christ.

What does that look like? In Philippians, the apostle Paul leads us on the path to peace: *Rejoice in what is true about God. Let prayer replace anxiety. Ask with a posture of gratitude.* And then how does peace come about? It comes through the person of Christ as He guards our hearts and minds as we surrender to Him. You see, we declutter our minds and hearts by bringing all our cares to Jesus, and when we are held by Him and trust in Him, He guards our minds and keeps the clutter at bay.

A FOCUS ON SELF COMPLICATES AND ADDS STRESS, BUT A FOCUS ON GOD'S FAITHFULNESS SIMPLIFIES AND FREES OUR HEARTS TO REJOICE.

grateful

...DO NOT
BE ANXIOUS ABOUT
ANYTHING...

a night focus

So to all of us who fall prey to stress and feel scattered: We can make our way through this Christmas season worn out and running on empty, or we can choose to prioritize gratitude by fixing our minds singularly on the peace of Christ. When we address our many anxieties by talking to God about them all with a heart of thanks, things like decor, menus, parties, or wish lists stop taking center stage as stressors. Trusting in God's care frees us up to take on a posture of peace and gratefulness. A focus on self complicates and adds stress, but a focus on God's faithfulness frees our hearts to rejoice with thanks. And when we rejoice in this season, we prepare Him room.

PONDER

What is one stressor you can replace today
with thanksgiving and prayer?

PRAISE

It Came Upon a Midnight Clear

PRAY

Dear Jesus, we trust You for all that clutters our minds
and hearts this day. We confess that our lack of peace
is so often tied to our lack of prayer, and our lack of
prayer is so often connected to a lack of thanksgiving
for what You have already done. So Lord, give us
thankful hearts. May we trust You for the peace that
guards our minds against anxious thoughts. Amen.

IT IS THE LORD
WHO GOES BEFORE YOU.
HE WILL BE WITH YOU;
HE WILL NOT LEAVE YOU
OR FORSAKE YOU.
DO NOT FEAR OR
BE DISMAYED.

DEUTERONOMY 31:8

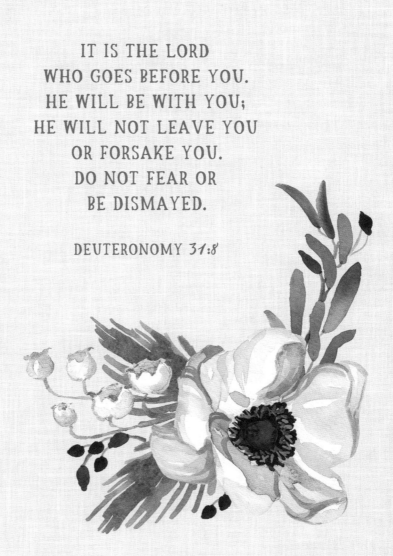

As for the rich in this present age, charge them not to be haughty, nor to set their hopes on the uncertainty of riches, but on God, who richly provides us with everything to enjoy. They are to do good, to be rich in good works, to be generous and ready to share, thus storing up treasure for themselves as a good foundation for the future, so that they may take hold of that which is truly life.

1 Timothy 6:17-19

Day 6

From Jealous to Joyful

What are you looking to for satisfaction? If that's a difficult question for you to answer, perhaps how you fill in the blank here will be more revealing: "All I want for Christmas is _____."
A new car? A day to yourself? Golf clubs? A new cell phone? A happy family? World peace? How would you fill in that space—that void—in your life? There's a longing in our hearts that even the magic of Christmastime can't satisfy. For most of us, what we really want—I mean *really* want—is to feel happy and joyful. Isn't that what we're seeking, after all, when we string up the lights, bake holiday favorites, look for the perfect gift, or reach out to the distant family member?

The hope for fulfillment of joy and a long-awaited promise is what led the wise men to follow the star to the birthplace of the Messiah. Even the oft-sung phrase in the beloved carol "O Holy Night" acknowledges this quest for joy and longing for satisfaction: "A thrill of hope, the weary world rejoices," we sing. The world to which Jesus came was curled up in a posture of weariness from endless striving, strife, and want. It longed to be free—to know the joy of relief.

Jesus, the long-awaited Messiah, came to a people oppressed by other nations and in bondage to their own sin. They wanted what other nations had—their own king. But God planned a more magnificent path to joy and freedom for His people than merely a ruler that could rival another; He purposed to give them eternal joy with a King whose kingdom will last forever. They hoped for so little compared to the treasure God intended for them. The same could be said of us.

WHERE YOU SET YOUR HOPE THIS
CHRISTMAS SEASON WILL
DETERMINE HOW YOU FIND JOY.

What about us in our longings this Christmas? Do we miss the joy of God's great eternal gift while hoping to secure something temporary to fix what's ailing us? It's easy to look to our left and right and believe something another person has will fill the void we feel. *A friend's new bike. A neighbor's house. Another's marriage. Someone else's career opportunities.* Nothing steals joy faster than jealousy and comparison—a longing for what doesn't satisfy. In a season so filled with stuff and earthly treasures, a posture of joy, formed by "that which is truly life," as we read in 1 Timothy, teaches us to long for heavenly treasure rather than the things of earth. "Christ Himself is our ultimate treasure. All else pales in comparison to Him," Randy Alcorn says, echoing a declaration the psalmist makes in Psalm 16:11:

Joyful

...TAKE HOLD OF THAT
WHICH IS TRULY LIFE.

You make known to me the path of life;
    in your presence there is fullness of joy;
    at your right hand are pleasures forevermore.

If joy is found in God's presence, and eternal pleasures known through His provisions, we have no reason to look and pine for anything else. Where you set your hope this Christmas season will determine how you find joy. We were made to know satisfaction in Christ alone; nothing else will do. This is the Christmas story, the gift that we will continue to unwrap during this Advent season.

PONDER

Take an inventory of what brings you joy. What do those things say about where you're setting your hope?

PRAISE

Joyful, Joyful, We Adore Thee

PRAY

Father, we confess that we are a people far too easily pleased. We don't grasp what riches of glory You've purchased for us through redemption. Help us to treasure You, to find our joy with You, and to be satisfied in You. Forgive us when we long for what others have, as if You've forgotten us in our need. May we trust You for the path of life—for what is truly life— and know joy in Your presence alone this Christmas. Amen.

JOYFUL, JOYFUL,
WE ADORE THEE
GOD OF GLORY,
LORD OF LOVE

HENRY VAN DYKE

As he considered these things, behold, an angel of the Lord appeared to him in a dream, saying, "Joseph son of David, do not fear to take Mary as your wife, for that which is conceived in her is from the Holy Spirit. She will bear a son, and you shall call his name Jesus, for he will save his people from their sins."

All this took place to fulfill what the Lord had spoken by the prophet:

"Behold, the virgin shall conceive and bear a son, and they shall call his name Immanuel" (which means God with us).

Matthew 1:20-23

WEEK TWO

God's
Promise

God's promise

The birth of Christ was no accident, surprise, or eleventh-hour rescue plan. It was God's promise all along. To think of Jesus as an afterthought to God's purposes and plans is to miss the wonder of the Redemption Story altogether—the opening chapter of which didn't take place at the manger, but in the heart of God from before time began.

How can we know that the Christmas story matters at all if we don't fully grasp our great need for a Savior? So many of us scurry about at Christmastime, hoping to find meaning in this season, when the true gift of the birth of Christ is found in unfathomable love in the heart of God. Try as we might, we can't muster up the feelings we want to feel at Christmas; we will experience the magnitude of Christmas only to the extent that we understand the grace and mercy of God's plan of redemption. The uncertainty and fear Joseph must have felt at the news of Mary's pregnancy turned to assurance when the angel of the Lord revealed the divine fulfillment of God's promise and plan. Joseph's circumstances didn't change; he simply trusted God to do the impossible. God's spoken promise, kept, removes our greatest uncertainties.

In the same way our heart posture determines how we begin to prepare Him room this Christmas, the full picture of God's promise of salvation invites us to see clearly what we're really celebrating in this season—and why it matters today in the midst of our uncertainties and impossible circumstances.

So, this is a story of hope...a story of rescue. This is a story that turns the posture of our hearts from *me* to *He.* This is a story we keep telling day after day, season after season, year after year— even after the last ornament has been put away. This is God's promise to His people and to all who will come to Him as He comes to us.

God saw everything that he had made,
and behold, it was very good.

Genesis 1:31

Day 7

A Relationship

Have you ever stood at the top of a mountain, or the ocean's edge, or deep in a redwood forest, or in the stillness of a winter blanket of snowfall, and wondered at God, "What is man that you are mindful of him?" (Psalm 8:4). *Who am I, God, that You hear me, know me, or meet me in my need?*

God's creation can draw out that wonder and humility in us that so often gets tangled up in our self-made confidence and sense of control. It can be hard to break away from our bustling lives to recognize clearly that *God is the creator of the universe. And I'm not.* "All things were created through Him, and apart from Him not one thing was created that has been created" (John 1:3 HCSB). How humbling to remember that nothing happens outside of God's care. How often do you remember, in the course of a day, that God is in full control of all that He's created? Likely, not enough.

It may not feel like it right now, but when God created the whole world, He called it good. Yes—the roaring ocean, the exquisite butterfly, the inkiest sky dotted with fireflies at night. A seahorse, a peacock, a sloth, an octopus, or an armadillo—designs only a creative God could imagine. But He didn't stop there. Our good and creative God also made you and me, unique and wonderfully different from anyone else in the world. He made beautifully rich skin tones and hair types. He made some to sing and some to dance, and some to be really good at math.

> ALL OF CREATION WAS FORMED, SHAPED, AND DESIGNED TO SHOW US HIS CHARACTER AND TO DECLARE HIS GLORY.

God made everything, and He called it good. He made our hearts to respond to music and He made tastebuds to experience all the flavors He has conceived. He made us to be different from the rest of creation; He made us for fellowship with Him. All of creation was formed, shaped, and designed to show us His character and to declare His glory. Elyse Fitzpatrick says it this way: "In His kindness, the Lord has revealed Himself to us. The invisible God who is incomprehensible to mankind has shown Himself through His creation (Romans 1:19-20). All we have to do is look around and we can learn something about Him. We see the order, the specificity, the grandeur, the sophistication of all that is, and we know that there is a God of immense wisdom, power and love."[3] God didn't create the universe out of boredom, but out of a desire to be Love to His created and have a relationship with us.

Creation was God's labor of love. It was His plan from the beginning to show His delight through creation and His faithfulness through fellowship with us, His image-bearers. God with us, through the birth of Christ, was His heart from the beginning—that we would be *with* Him. The Jesus

a
Relationship

IN THE BEGINNING, GOD
CREATED THE HEAVENS
AND THE EARTH.

created
for Him

we find in the manger is indeed Immanuel, *God with us*, but God demonstrated His presence and desire to be with us from the very start of creation.

Creation is forever connected to the Christmas story because it is there that God reveals His heart for us, His children. It is there we find the unhindered fellowship He intended for men and women to have with Him—a tender and intimate relationship given to no other part of creation. And so, as we prepare Him room this Advent season, don't forget where it all began: God and His creation, good and made to walk with Him.

When we start here, we begin to discover that Christmas—the story of *God with us*—is not about us, but about the heart of God. And if we know nothing else, this is enough: that our Creator God loves us and created us for Himself. Does that frame the anticipation of Christmas in a new way for you?

PONDER

What aspects of creation remind you of God's care?

PRAISE

O Little Town of Bethlehem

PRAY

Creator God, we're brought low when we consider all
that You've done and all the ways that You continue
to hold all things together. When we feel alone in this
world, remind us that You created us for relationship
and nearness to You. Lord, may we know the
significance of that invitation this Christmas season.

WHOM HAVE I IN
HEAVEN BUT YOU?
AND THERE IS NOTHING
ON EARTH THAT I
DESIRE BESIDES YOU.

PSALM 73:25

None is righteous, no, not one; no one
understands; no one seeks for God. All have
turned aside; together they have become
worthless; no one does good, not even one.

Romans 3:10-12

Day 8

A Wonderful Savior

Have you stopped to consider this lately: We will not recognize the birth of Christ as a miraculous gift of promise until we realize the miserable condition of desperation we would all know otherwise.

If your house or bedroom were filthy from months and months of neglect—with clothes everywhere, dirty dishes and silverware stacked on the table, a thick layer of dust coating every surface, and cockroaches or mouse droppings beneath the furniture (eww!)—you would feel so desperate and buried from the weight of the mess you had made. Shame, embarrassment, and doubt would creep in and keep you from letting anyone see the truth behind closed doors.

But what if, by some miracle, someone loved you enough to come into your impossible mess and not only help you with the problem, but take it on in its entirety? If you left and came back home hours (days?) later to a sparkling clean home, you'd likely weep tears of joy because the condition you were stuck in for so long had been lifted, done away with, and reset to what it should have been all along.

WE CAN'T KNOW THE WONDER OF CHRISTMAS WITHOUT TASTING OF OUR DESPERATION WITHOUT HIM.

So as harsh as Romans 3 may sound to us, the apostle Paul tells the truth we need to hear about our condition without Christ. We were stuck in our rebellion and depravity before a holy God on account of our sin. Until Jesus came. This is the very gift of Christmas—God coming into our impossible mess and making a way out of our despair.

We can't know the wonder of Christmas without tasting of our desperation without Him. Many know Christmas to be a difficult time of loss, sadness, or unmet longings in their hearts. Pain doesn't take a holiday. Be it sickness, death, separation, conflict, or sadness, sin is the source of the brokenness we all feel this side of heaven. Don't be surprised when sin causes pain and sadness, even at Christmastime. The sin that causes us to snap at family members when things don't go our way. The sin that makes us point out others' mistakes while hiding our own. The sin that keeps us spiraling downward in worry and doubt. The sin that makes us love ourselves more than we love God. It's the really bad news that makes the really good news so sweet.

But what if the desperation caused by our sinful nature drives us to truly desire the Christ of Christmas? What if the brokenness brought about by sin causes us to prepare Him room where once only rebellion dwelt? God created us for fellowship with Him. We broke that fellowship by trusting in ourselves instead of God when Adam and Eve believed they knew better than their Creator.

a
Wonderful
Savior

NONE IS RIGHTEOUS,
NO NOT ONE...

Christmas is a reminder that there is no repair for our despair apart from our wonderful Savior, Jesus, the Messiah. We won't know the sweetness of a Savior if we don't realize how much we need rescuing. No wonder Isaac Watts could pen these words in "Joy to the World": "No more let sins and sorrows grow, nor thorns infest the ground; He comes to make His blessings flow far as the curse is found." No matter how joyous the Christmas season, it's still but a shadow of the eternal joy we have as broken people who are restored—as those who will one day feast and celebrate in God's presence in eternity.

Christmas is the celebration of God's promise to crush the curse through His Son, Christ, born as a baby to live among us. No longer bound by sin and death, we who were once sent from God's presence can fellowship with Him again in spite of our sin—because of a perfect and wonderful Savior.

PONDER

Confess your need for Jesus, especially in this season. What are you tempted to love more than Him? That's the sin Jesus came to free you from.

PRAISE

Let All Mortal Flesh Keep Silence

PRAY

Lord, the weight of our sin would crush us if not for Jesus.
We, too, like Adam and Eve, have chosen our own way,
thinking we know better than You. We need a Savior. So
help us to see the worthlessness of our sin as we prepare
our hearts during this Advent season, and to die to that
which You came to destroy. May we have awareness of
our sin and show gratitude for Your grace. Amen.

THE STING OF DEATH IS SIN,
AND THE POWER OF SIN IS THE LAW.
BUT THANKS BE TO GOD,
WHO GIVES US THE VICTORY
THROUGH OUR LORD JESUS CHRIST.

1 CORINTHIANS 15:56-57

Have mercy on me, O God,
    according to your steadfast love;
according to your abundant mercy
    blot out my transgressions.
Wash me thoroughly from my iniquity,
    and cleanse me from my sin!

For I know my transgressions,
    and my sin is ever before me.
Against you, you only, have I sinned
    and done what is evil in your sight,
so that you may be justified in your words
    and blameless in your judgment.
Behold, I was brought forth in iniquity,
    and in sin did my mother conceive me.
Behold, you delight in truth in the inward being,
    and you teach me wisdom in the secret heart.

Psalm 51:1-6

Day 9

A Merciful God

When David penned these words in Psalm 51, he was a man deeply aware of his own sin. He had violated a woman who was not his wife, murdered her husband, and cowardly misused his role as a king. And yet, in his heart, he knew his greatest violation was against God. He knew he had broken his relationship with the Lord. David's heart was in ruin...because sin never delivers on its promises.

But God keeps His promises. And when sin entered the world and caused ruin in every way possible, rescue was already in the mind of God, and the course of redemption was already set.

Have you ever considered the thought that God could've met the curse of sin with its remedy right away, like an instant Band-Aid on a wound? But He didn't. He allowed all of us to feel the pain and consequences of sin so that we might surrender. God isn't interested in simply fixing us; He wants our hearts. He desires hearts *fixed* on Him.

The ruin caused by sin and our inability to make things right with God were always meant to lead us to surrender. And God's aim is specific. He doesn't desire that we throw up our hands and give up in frustration, but that we lay down all our efforts in humility before Him, a merciful Father. Thomas Brooks wrote, "Nothing humbles and breaks the heart of a sinner like mercy and love." Only those who are heartbroken seek to have their hearts mended. And this surrender is the very place where God meets us with hope.

Do you ever struggle to experience the hope of Christmas because you're stuck in the muck and mire of sinful choices and life patterns? Perhaps, like David, you've made such painful mistakes that you wonder whether you can come to the Lord at all. If your heart hurts from the ways you've pursued happiness apart from God, you are in the perfect place to meet God's mercy with surrender.

> NO SIN IS TOO GREAT, NO HEART TOO HARD TO CALL UPON THE MERCY OF GOD AND FIND HIS LOVE STEADY AND TRUE.

You were created to fellowship with God. Sin broke the intimacy and the freedom intended for you in His presence. But God didn't leave you in that brokenness; instead, He allowed you to feel the desperation of that brokenness so that you might long for a Savior.

Is that your longing? Then surrender. Even now, especially now...at Christmas. No sin is too great, no heart is too hard to call upon the mercy of God and find His love steady and true.

Do you already have the gift of salvation but need to release your ideas of self-assurance and return to your loving Savior in humility? Have you,

a
Merciful God

HAVE MERCY
ON ME, O GOD...

amidst all the busyness of life, forgotten that Jesus desires your surrender more than your hard work or perfect track record? He's after your heart.

As we surrender in this Advent season and seek Jesus, we'll discover the miracle of Christmas: That while we wander on our windy roads to find Him, Jesus has already come to us. Our God didn't wait for us to perfectly surrender before He came to perfectly save. The invitation is ours and waiting for us, even now.

PONDER

How has God been merciful to you?
How has that mercy led you to Jesus?

PRAISE

We Three Kings of Orient Are

PRAY

Father, we thank You for seeking us out in our sin even before we knew to seek You. Your love and mercy draw us near, and as Your Word says, "While we were still sinners, Christ died for us" (Romans 5:8). Help us to let that sink in today, that we might be amazed at Your kindness. And when we forget, and sin threatens to keep us from coming to You, remind us that You've already come to us. Thank You for Christ; thank You for the promise of redemption. We surrender...and find our hope in You alone. Amen.

THE LORD IS MERCIFUL
AND GRACIOUS, SLOW TO
ANGER AND ABOUNDING
IN STEADFAST LOVE.

PSALM 103:8

Zechariah was filled with the Holy Spirit and prophesied, saying,

> "Blessed be the Lord God of Israel, for he has visited and redeemed his people and has raised up a horn of salvation for us in the house of his servant David...And you, child, will be called the prophet of the Most High; for you will go before the Lord to prepare his ways, to give knowledge of salvation to his people in the forgiveness of their sins, because of the tender mercy of our God."

Luke 1:67-78

Day 10

A Coming Messiah

Because of the tender mercy of our God rightly describes the way God carried out His promise to save His people. God's plan was so carefully and compassionately executed that He even sent John the Baptist ahead of Jesus to "prepare his ways, to give knowledge of salvation to his people in the forgiveness of their sins." God didn't want His people to miss this; His prescription for the very brokenness that ailed them was His Son, Christ—who would restore all who received and believed in Him to fellowship with Himself.

If you were suffering from an illness with seemingly no cure, you would be desperate to not only receive the correct diagnosis, but also news of any effective remedy for your condition. If there was a cure for a deadly virus, you would want to know. If there was a way to destroy cancer once and for all, you would be ready for it. And if the remedy was paid for and cost nothing but a willingness to come, you would be crazy to not receive it. Right? God's people and all of creation ached with longing for sin's remedy. They tried everything to no avail; there was no cure whatsoever for man's brokenness.

God waited for the time He appointed in history—the exact moment chosen to fulfill His promise—and declared, "Hope has come."

And that hope was Jesus, born to do what we could not. Jesus was born through divine means, lived a sinless life, walked among us to show compassion, to teach, to be a friend, to be an example, and to carry out His Father's will. He was not one of us but came among us that we might know the presence of God in a tangible way. Jesus was the Promised One who would crush the serpent's head—the promise from the beginning. You see, the miracle of Christmas was not simply the virgin birth; the miracle was that God made good on His promise to rescue His people. And He did it Himself, choosing to come in the feeble frame of a man on earth. God's promise wasn't just carried out to completion, it was carried out in love and compassion.

JESUS WAS NOT BORN TO STAY IN A MANGER; HE WAS BORN TO GO TO THE CROSS.

When you see an infant lying in a manger this Christmas—a popular visual image representing the miraculous story in Scripture—don't let your affections remain there. Jesus is more than a baby, more than a beautiful miracle in a harsh world. He is more than a familiar figure sung about in festive tunes. Jesus is God with us—Immanuel, just as the angel of the Lord told Joseph.

Christmas and the anticipation of Jesus Christ, our Messiah, is precious only to the degree that we are desperate to find freedom from what ails us.

a Coming
Messiah

...GIVE KNOWLEDGE
OF SALVATION TO
HIS PEOPLE...

the Promised One

Jesus was not born to stay in a manger; He was born to go to the cross. And this Jesus—He is the answer we have been longing for.

PONDER

What problems or dissatisfaction
have you been trying to fix on your own?

PRAISE

Away in a Manger

PRAY

God, we thank You for Your Son, Jesus, whom You sent
to save us from ourselves. Forgive us for the ways we
forget that He alone saves us—not our feel-good fixes
or strategic solutions. We need a Savior, and You've
made a way for us to be saved. Thank You for Jesus
and what His birth, life, death, and resurrection mean
for those who receive Him as the Messiah. Help us
believe, Lord. And help us in our unbelief. Amen.

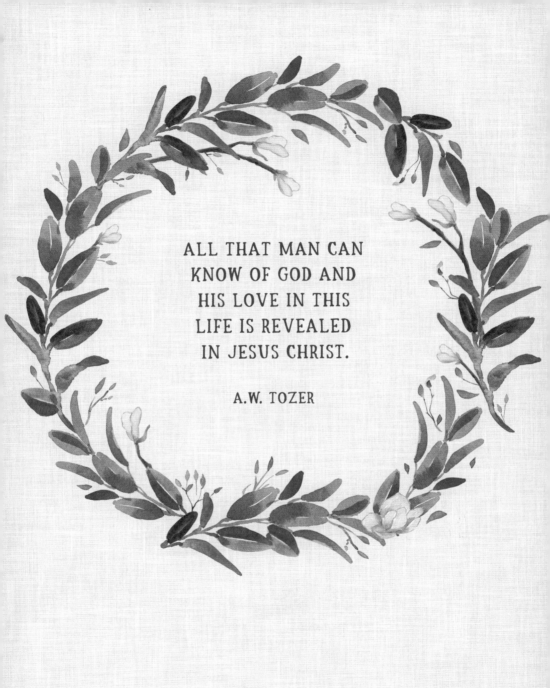

ALL THAT MAN CAN
KNOW OF GOD AND
HIS LOVE IN THIS
LIFE IS REVEALED
IN JESUS CHRIST.

A.W. TOZER

God, being rich in mercy, because of the great love with which he loved us, even when we were dead in our trespasses, made us alive together with Christ—by grace you have been saved—and raised us up with him and seated us with him in the heavenly places in Christ Jesus, so that in the coming ages he might show the immeasurable riches of his grace in kindness toward us in Christ Jesus. For by grace you have been saved through faith. And this is not your own doing; it is the gift of God, not a result of works, so that no one may boast. For we are his workmanship, created in Christ Jesus for good works, which God prepared beforehand, that we should walk in them.

Ephesians 2:4-10

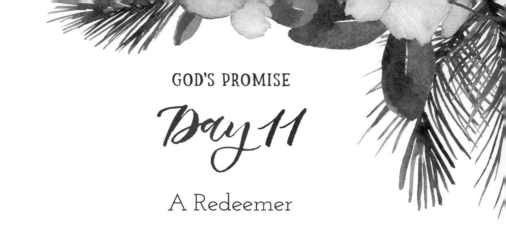

GOD'S PROMISE

Day 11

A Redeemer

To walk through a shopping mall during this season is to get the impression Christmas is the most important holiday in the Western world. And with all the travel, gift-buying, events, and concerts...perhaps it is, but not for the reasons we as Christ-followers pause to celebrate. If Jesus is the reason for the season, then the resurrection is really the most life-changing event we can celebrate. The baby Jesus born to Mary and Joseph in Bethlehem is truly a miracle only because He was the promised Messiah. Without the cross, the baby in the manger is but novel and fascinating, not life-changing.

And what we long for right now, in the midst of the hustle, the mess, and the mundane, is *life-changing*. If we're honest, it's not a patch-up job we hope to make room for in this season; we want real change. We want the Christmas miracle to change our lives and not just our wallets as we meet the demands of *more* gifts, *more* events, *more* parties, *more, more, more*. Perhaps when we struggle to experience that kind of heart change at Christmas it is because we've left the resurrection out of our celebration of the incarnation.

The gospel is the good news for the weary soul only because Jesus came, died, and rose again.

The weary world in Jesus' day expected a savior who would lead them to conquer other nations. They failed to recognize that Jesus came to conquer a greater enemy—the bondage of sin and death. Jesus came to live the sinless life we could not live, to pay the price for our sin that we couldn't pay, and to rise again so that we might be *born* again into new life with the Father—no longer as enemies but as beloved children. They couldn't grasp the eternal victory of redemption through Christ amidst their fixation to win earthly wars.

BECAUSE OF THE CROSS, NOTHING IS NOR WILL EVER BE THE SAME.

The resurrection calls us to look beyond the here and now—the temporary solutions we seek when we try to save ourselves by our own efforts. What earthly concern are you so fixated on right now that you may be missing the resurrection hope you have in Christ?

Christmas is the beginning of the road to redemption. Because Jesus didn't simply come as a baby but died and rose again as our Redeemer, we are raised up to new life with Him when we receive God's gracious gift of salvation. He fulfilled this promise so that we might be restored and reconciled to our Creator God. The resurrection is the hinge of history. Because of the cross, nothing is nor will ever be the same.

a Redeemer

...RAISED US UP WITH
HIM AND SEATED US
WITH HIM...

alive in Him

PONDER

In what ways do you try to "save" yourself by being
better or more cleaned up? Ask the Lord to help you
put your trust in His work of redemption instead.

PRAISE

Go, Tell It on the Mountain

PRAY

Lord Jesus, we celebrate the wonder of Your birth
because of Your sacrifice at the cross. Remind us in this
season to hope in Your resurrection. Because You are
alive, we can be born again. Help us to die to what is
temporary and to live for what is eternal. Amen.

'TIS MERCY ALL,
IMMENSE AND FREE;
FOR O MY GOD,
IT FOUND OUT ME.
AMAZING LOVE!
HOW CAN IT BE
THAT THOU, MY GOD,
SHOULD DIE FOR ME!

CHARLES WESLEY

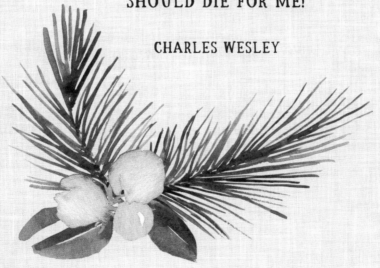

We are debtors, not to the flesh, to live according to the flesh. For if you live according to the flesh you will die, but if by the Spirit you put to death the deeds of the body, you will live. For all who are led by the Spirit of God are sons of God. For you did not receive the spirit of slavery to fall back into fear, but you have received the Spirit of adoption as sons, by whom we cry, "Abba! Father!" The Spirit himself bears witness with our spirit that we are children of God, and if children, then heirs—heirs of God and fellow heirs with Christ, provided we suffer with him in order that we may also be glorified with him.

Romans 8:12-17

Day 12

A Transformed Life

It's amusing to see the ways children imitate parents, whether they intend to or not. When they're young, little girls try on their mother's prettiest dresses and little boys try and wear their dad's tool belt. Kids imitate their parents' laughs and sometimes even the way they walk. How many times have you caught yourself doing something you've seen your parents do? But as we get older, the imitation decreases with our proximity to our parents. You can't as easily imitate from a distance.

This is why, after His resurrection, Jesus promised us the Holy Spirit as our ever-present help and God's presence in our lives. When we receive Christ, we invite the work of the gospel to transform our lives. This transforming work is done by the Holy Spirit, who dwells in us. The proximity of God's presence and the nearness of His Word—His love letter to us—gives us access and the ability to imitate our heavenly Father. Even children who once were far off, rebellious, and unwilling to follow in their Father's steps are brought near because of Jesus and are given the capacity to live according to their new identities in Christ—as sons and daughters of God.

WHEN WE PREPARE HIM ROOM AT CHRISTMAS, WE MAKE ROOM FOR A LIFETIME IN HIS PRESENCE.

If the idea of Immanuel—God with us—blows your mind, it should. But more stunning than even the birth of Christ is the mystery of the Savior's presence forever with us, wherever we go, through the Spirit. *God with us* wasn't one event on Christmas Day, or one lifetime in the 33 years that Jesus walked the earth. *God with us* is forevermore in the lives of those who receive Him as Savior and King. Do you see how God's promise of rescue far outshines a candlelight service or a season of festivities? When we prepare Him room at Christmas, we make room for a lifetime in His presence. Jesus doesn't want our partial attention during the month of December; He wants our hearts every day of every year. He wants us to be transformed.

Change can and will happen right where you are when you abide in Christ. To abide means to dwell with Him as He dwells in you. Change happens when we imitate Christ. And you know what? He is our only perfect example. The fruit of redemption is not a better set of circumstances or an improved outlook; it is a changed life. This is God's promise of redemption. When we become recipients of this promise, we are not only transformed in our true identities, we are given an entirely new eternal family to belong to.

So as we seek to celebrate Christ's birth in this season, let's start by celebrating the new birth granted to us when we trust in Him. The true gift of Jesus is the invitation to become sons and daughters in the kingdom of God.

More than simply better circumstances or a new outlook, our new life in Christ brings us an entirely new identity: We are no longer enemies or fearful outsiders, but heirs with Christ, who have been brought near. We

a *Transformed Life*

FOR ALL WHO
ARE LED BY THE SPIRIT OF
GOD ARE SONS OF GOD.

Child of God

were made to reflect Him, and He is worthy of that imitation. So rejoice! In Christ, we've been restored to the fellowship we were made for with our heavenly Father—a restoration planned by God in eternity past, and fulfilled in Jesus, the promised Messiah.

PONDER
Recount the ways Jesus has transformed your life.

PRAISE
O Come, O Come, Emmanuel

PRAY
Dear God, You are our only means of change. We long to be more like You. Whenever we are tempted to forget our new identity in Christ, remind us through Your Word that we are forgiven and free, loved and welcomed. Teach us to follow in Your steps and to walk in a manner worthy of You. Amen.

WE ALL, WITH UNVEILED FACE,
BEHOLDING THE GLORY OF THE LORD,
ARE BEING TRANSFORMED INTO THE
SAME IMAGE FROM ONE DEGREE OF
GLORY TO ANOTHER. FOR THIS COMES
FROM THE LORD WHO IS THE SPIRIT.

2 CORINTHIANS 3:18

In the same region there were shepherds out in the field, keeping watch over their flock by night. And an angel of the Lord appeared to them, and the glory of the Lord shone around them, and they were filled with great fear. And the angel said to them, "Fear not, for behold, I bring you good news of great joy that will be for all the people. For unto you is born this day in the city of David a Savior, who is Christ the Lord. And this will be a sign for you: you will find a baby wrapped in swaddling cloths and lying in a manger." And suddenly there was with the angel a multitude of the heavenly host praising God and saying,

"Glory to God in the highest,
   and on earth peace among those with
   whom he is pleased!"

When the angels went away from them into heaven, the shepherds said to one another, "Let us go over to Bethlehem and see this thing that has happened, which the Lord has made known to us."

Luke 2:8-15

WEEK THREE

Our response

WEEK THREE

Our response

No one who truly encounters Jesus Christ remains unchanged.

The birth of Jesus broke the 400 years of silence between God and man—a time when God prepared nations, peoples, and hearts for the imminent arrival of the Savior. Having heard the prophecies and the stories of God's mighty works, the Jewish people no doubt began to wonder, with each passing generation and no Messiah, if they heard incorrectly.

But just as He promised, predicted, and orchestrated, God sent Jesus at the appointed time in history. The long-awaited event was unadorned but for the worshipful hearts that gathered around. It was unspectacular to any unsuspecting onlooker; but to those who knew what God had done, it was a miracle. Most wondrous of all is that God didn't send a powerful ruler, an intelligent strategist, or a moral hero to lead the way. God sent Himself to make a way where there was no way.

For all of us on the other side of the cross—who have been given the full picture of God's promises fulfilled—Christmas is more than sentimentality, tradition, or a family celebration. It is a gift, described by Peter, as "things into which angels long to look" (1 Peter 1:12). What we have as the answer for our deepest longings is that which those who lived long before the cross ached to know in full.

You see, such a tremendous gift given through Christ, promised by God, compels a response. The wise men and the shepherds weren't forced to come celebrate the birth of Jesus. They didn't go under obligation and they didn't muster up the right attitude upon witnessing this baby born in a manger. The first to celebrate the birth of Jesus were compelled to do so and worship with their treasures, their time, their hearts, and their praise. They believed and acted accordingly.

We're invited to do the same. The fulfilled promise of the birth of Christ doesn't just cause us to celebrate during the holiday season; it compels us to respond with our entire lives.

By the word of the LORD the heavens were made,
  and by the breath of his mouth all their host.
He gathers the waters of the sea as a heap;
  he puts the deeps in storehouses.

Let all the earth fear the LORD;
  let all the inhabitants of the world stand in awe of him!
For he spoke, and it came to be;
  he commanded, and it stood firm.

Psalm 33:6-9

Day 13

Awe + Wonder

Miracles happen every day.

They may not look like the literal parting of the Red Sea, but God makes a way through the wilderness each and every day of our lives—starting, first and foremost, with the way of salvation through the promised Savior of the world, Jesus of Nazareth. The psalmist didn't know the wonders of the virgin birth and the sinless life, burial, and resurrection of Christ, but he experienced a profound sense of awe when he considered God's handiwork as the Creator who spoke the world into existence. Day by day, God continues to hold the world together by His power. From the sun that calls this day into order, piercing through the darkest night, to the blazing sunset that lingers past the day's toils, God still puts His power and sovereign care on display. He still calls us to respond with wonder and awe.

I heard the story of how, during the Christmas season of 1995, a team of scientists decided to point the Hubble Space Telescope at a small, starless spot of sky and take pictures of it—*for ten days*, despite the enormity of the cost to investigate something that seemed apparently unspectacular. This is what they discovered: "Hubble's images delighted the astronomical community. Formally known as the Hubble Deep Field, the 'blank' spot contained some 3,000 galaxies of all shapes, colors, and sizes, like presents under the tree on Christmas morning."[4] If that causes you to marvel, it should. God and His design for us is so much more complex and extravagant than we know. In the dizzying array of technology and man-made creations, it's easy to be in awe of the work of our own hands, forgetting the very breath we breathe is a gift from God.

So, does this Christmas season find you full of awe and wonder, or jaded from the numbing strain of busyness? It's hard to be full of praise and adoration when we are filled with worry and self-striving.

THE MIRACLE OF CHRISTMAS IS IN THIS: THAT A HOLY GOD MADE A WAY FOR ALL WHO BELIEVE TO COME TO HIM... BY FIRST COMING TO US.

Are you tempted to discount the seemingly unremarkable corners of your life? What if the God of wonders is at work in ways more than you can possibly imagine?

The true miracle of Christmas isn't simply the virgin birth; it's much greater than even such an impossibility. No, the miracle of Christmas is in this: that a holy God made a way for all who believe to come to Him...by first coming to us. Let that sink in. God's promises, fulfilled by God Himself, are more than remarkable; they merit a response—not to get busy, but to fall down in reverence and awe for our great God.

Awe + Wonder

...STAND IN AWE
OF HIM!

And for this great love and pursuit from the Father, He doesn't seek a response of show or extravagance; He desires our surrendered praise. O, that we might bow low and respond with lifted hearts, declaring, "You are God Almighty, and we stand in awe of You."

PONDER

What stirs up awe and wonder in your soul?

PRAISE

O Come, All Ye Faithful

PRAY

Father, You are worthy of our praise. When we consider Your faithfulness through the works of Your hands, through the gift of Your Son, and through the ways You care for us day by day, we're humbled and we remember once again: You are God and we are not. Lord, forgive us for the ways we try to steal Your glory and trust in ourselves. You draw near to us each day and put on display the ways You are still sovereign and good. May we give You the adoration and praise You deserve—not just this Christmas season, but each and every day. Amen.

PRAISE IS A SOUL
IN FLOWER.

THOMAS WATSON

Faith is the assurance of things hoped for,
the conviction of things not seen.

Hebrews 11:1

Day 14

Faith

Chances are, even in this very moment, you are surrounded by the sights of the Christmas season. Twinkling lights, your favorite ornament, snow falling gently, rolls of gilded gift wrap and reams of ribbon, the nativity collection that comes out every December...the obnoxiously massive blow-up Frosty the Snowman in your neighbor's front yard. We experience so much of the season visually.

If you are able to see, you've likely taken your sight for granted. We perceive, observe, and absorb all that comes to us visually thanks to eyes that see, naturally or with correction. Our ability to interpret the world around us through sight is a gift we often overlook in the same way we can underestimate the gift of faith. We walk around, largely unaware that everything we take in from our surroundings and circumstances is directly affected by how well our eyes work...and in the case of spiritual sight, how clearly we see through our eyes of faith. If our physical eyes are the organ for sight, faith is the organ of perception for things unseen—for the trials you don't understand, the suffering you didn't anticipate, the change you don't grasp the purpose of. We cannot walk in the truth of God's love and redemption of our souls without exercising the muscle of belief and the organ of faith.[5] "By grace you have been saved through faith. And this is not your own doing; it is the gift of God" (Ephesians 2:8). Faith is a gift from the Lord that enables us to believe and trust in Him. When we respond in faith, we acknowledge all that is true of who God is and who He says we are, and we ask Him for the grace to walk in that truth. More than a fleeting feeling, faith connects what we know with how we believe and shapes our walk of obedience to God.

> THE STARTING POINT OF GREATER
> FAITH IS ALWAYS GREATER RELIANCE
> ON THE GIVER OF FAITH.

Perhaps this season finds you lacking faith or the ability to perceive with confidence through your weary eyes of doubt. The answer isn't to muster up the feelings of faith or a pep-rally assurance that you can "let go and let God." No, the true response of faith is forged from the fires of fear, despair, weariness, and insecurity. Faith is a God-given gift we then nurture and exercise. The starting point of greater faith is always greater reliance on the Giver of faith. We echo the desire for belief as we make the same plea given by the father of the son Jesus healed: "I believe; help my unbelief!" (Mark 9:24).

One of the ways we strengthen, exercise, and adjust the organ of faith is by aligning that faith with the truth from God's Word. Truth is how we measure whether we are walking according to our own wisdom or according to God's. Faith allows us to process and believe that truth so that it changes us.[6] It's tempting to reduce faith to a courageous act, a big-hearted feeling of goodwill, or a Christmas-induced return to the "old-time religion." Resist

Faith

...FAITH IS THE ASSURANCE
OF THINGS HOPED FOR...

these insufficient pictures of faith, as they will only leave you unsatisfied, disappointed, and unchanged. These are the results you can expect when you look to yourself, a magical feeling, or a holiday season as your source for faith. But if, instead, you look to Jesus—and respond in belief to what He says He has done to save you—the result of that response is the gift of faith. The gifts of the season are plentiful, but none quite compare to the blessing it is to grasp and unwrap what He has prepared for you.

PONDER

How has God increased your faith in times when
your circumstances haven't changed?

PRAISE

The First Noel

PRAY

Dear Father, we thank You for the gift of faith, without
which we could not know You, trust You, or draw
near to Your heart. Help us to exercise our faith by
returning to Your Word, again and again, instead
of our own wisdom. And as we do, Lord, grow our
faith that we might trust You more. Amen.

FAITH MAKES
INVISIBLE THINGS VISIBLE,
ABSENT THINGS PRESENT,
AND THINGS THAT ARE
VERY FAR OFF TO BE VERY
NEAR TO THE SOUL.

THOMAS BROOKS

What God foretold by the mouth of all the prophets, that his Christ would suffer, he thus fulfilled. Repent therefore, and turn back, that your sins may be blotted out, that times of refreshing may come from the presence of the Lord, and that he may send the Christ appointed for you, Jesus, whom heaven must receive until the time for restoring all the things about which God spoke by the mouth of his holy prophets long ago.

Acts 3:18-21

Day 15

Repentance

There's nothing like finding out that you've been on the wrong road, headed to a destination you didn't intend to go to. These days, with navigation in our cars and the map apps on our phones, it's harder to lose your way. But no one, after realizing that he or she has taken the wrong road, chooses to continue down a path that won't get them where they want to go. Awareness of waywardness bids a response...a change of course.

When God fulfilled His promise for an awaited Savior through Jesus, He did so to show the way back to Him. Jesus taught, demonstrated, and declared again and again that He was the one true Way. God's patience and mercy in sending Christ was a kindness "meant to lead you to repentance" (Romans 2:4). Repentance is a turning—a complete 180 degrees—from the path you're on. Just as we might turn around and change course when we know we're going the wrong way, we are called to repent and turn from our sin...the path leading to destruction, emptiness, and pain.

This requires not just turning *from* the wrong way but turning *to* the right path. Paul and Barnabas said it this way in Acts 14:15 when they confronted the pagan crowds in Lystra: "You should turn from these vain things to a living God, who made the heaven and the earth and the sea and all that is in them." We turn to the holy God when we realize we've been blind to the truth.

> GOD'S GREATNESS AND MAJESTY
> CALL US TO DEPART FROM
> OUR OWN WAY AND TO WORSHIP HIM.

Repentance is a transformed heart that declares that God is God and we are not, and turns from believing otherwise. Repentance is an active response to what we come to believe in our hearts. If we believe we have no hope apart from Jesus, we will surrender our self-made efforts at assurance. If we believe His plan for salvation, we will turn from our own solutions. If we believe God's mercy welcomes us, we'll turn from the emptiness we're in and run to Him. God's greatness and majesty call us to depart from our own way and to worship Him. Just as the crowds in Lystra were told to turn from the worship of false gods to the worship of the one true God, we now have the roadmap for repentance through the Word of God—to turn from our false gods of self-fulfillment and self-sufficiency.

The manger scene—the very condescension of a holy God to earth—is a declaration that God took extreme measures to meet us in the midst of our waywardness and to personally deliver us from the path to destruction. Our hope at Christmas is not that we might have temporary fixes to our troubles, but that we would know the permanent change that occurs when we meet the Savior, Jesus Christ, and repent.

Repentance

REPENT THEREFORE,

AND TURN BACK...

repent

Every "Hallelujah!" of Christmas begins with surrender and a turning. There's no rejoicing until we respond in repentance.

PONDER

Where is God calling you to repentance as you declare His faithfulness in your life?

PRAISE

Silent Night, Holy Night

PRAY

Father God, Your mercy compels us to come near and lay down our striving and self-reliance. Your kindness leads us to repentance. The truth is, we wouldn't come otherwise, so thank You. Help us to rightly recognize the course we're on, and where we've been wayward. We pray that You will align our hearts with the hope of redemption as we turn from our sin. Thank You for coming into our midst and showing us the way back to You. Amen.

THE BROKEN SPIRIT AND
THE CONTRITE HEART
ARE THE ABIDING MARKS
OF THE BELIEVING SOUL.

JOHN MURRAY

As you received Christ Jesus the Lord, so walk in him, rooted and built up in him and established in the faith, just as you were taught, abounding in thanksgiving.

Colossians 2:6-7

Day 16

Thanksgiving

Have you noticed how easy it is to complain, feel discontent, or struggle with gratitude during the Christmas season when we've just spent deliberate time giving thanks a few weeks earlier on Thanksgiving? If it feels like being grateful takes earnest effort, it should. Because of sin, our hearts are hardwired for self-centeredness and idolatry.

Left to ourselves, we will always think we are lacking and don't have quite enough...when we notice someone else's holiday decor, when a friend or sibling receives a gift we wish was ours, when another family's photos look blissful while we are struggling in our own homes. We are not called to fake a grin through the aching in our hearts, but we *are* called to set our hope on Jesus, the Giver of all that we need:

> He who supplies seed to the sower and bread for food will supply and multiply your seed for sowing and increase the harvest of your righteousness. You will be enriched in every way to be generous in every way, which through us will produce thanksgiving to God (2 Corinthians 9:10-11).

When we place our attention on all that's been granted us through Jesus, our hearts change. A response to God's gifts with thanksgiving redirects our hearts and minds:

> Do not be anxious about anything, but in everything by prayer and supplication with thanksgiving let your requests be made known to God. And the peace of God, which surpasses all understanding, will guard your hearts and your minds in Christ Jesus (Philippians 4:6-7).

Peace on earth...the peace we all say we want at Christmas, and year 'round, is a gift that comes through trusting Jesus to provide what we cannot. True peace with God is the good news of the gospel, but continuing peace of mind—the peace that surpasses understanding—is the byproduct of trusting God through prayer and thanksgiving.

WHEN OUR HOPE
IS SECURE IN JESUS,
WE CAN GIVE THANKS
IN ANY SEASON.

Paul tells us in Colossians that this kind of thanksgiving can abound in our lives. How? How can we abound in thanksgiving when we are so aware of the many deficiencies, difficulties, and disappointments in our lives? Let's look again to what Paul tells us in Colossians 2:

> As you received Christ Jesus the Lord, so walk in him, rooted and built up in him and established in the faith, just as you were taught, abounding in thanksgiving (verses 6-7).

Thanksgiving

...ABOUNDING IN
THANKSGIVING.

give thanks

Ah, there it is: *rooted and built up in Him and established in the faith.*

Our response of thanksgiving increases only as our roots in the truths of God's Word deepen. Thanksgiving is like the shoots and branches from a plant firmly rooted in the good news of the gospel.

So as the Advent season stirs up gratitude for family, friends, and our many good gifts, let the "abounding in thanksgiving" Paul speaks of result from being rooted through faith in Jesus Christ—the Jesus who didn't merely come as a baby, but delivered as Savior of the world. When our hope is secure in Jesus, we can give thanks in any season.

PONDER

What are you most grateful for during this Advent season?

PRAISE

Sing We Now of Christmas

PRAY

Dear Father, we give thanks for all that You have done. We thank You for Jesus and His work on the cross on our behalf. We thank You that we are not asked to rescue ourselves through good works or good intentions. Thank You for being a merciful God who lavished grace upon us when we were undeserving. Because of Your steadfast love that pursues us, even now, we give back to You our sacrifice of praise. We want to respond with thanksgiving. Help us, Lord, to live as we truly are in Christ—immeasurably blessed.

LET YOUR GRATITUDE
COMPEL YOU IN
EVERYTHING YOU
DO FOR JESUS.

C.H. SPURGEON

A new commandment I give to you, that you love one another: just as I have loved you, you also are to love one another. By this all people will know that you are my disciples, if you have love for one another.

John 13:34-35

Day 17

Love

February is the month we expect to see hearts and celebrations of love, but if we read God's Word as He intended, Christmas and the resurrection of Christ would be equally love-laden celebrations of a love so grand, so immeasurable that even the most elaborate paper-cut hearts and the most sparkling diamonds could not compare. Christmas marks the beginning of Christ's walk of love on earth, and the resurrection the final act of love in His earthly life.

As we continue in this Advent season, remembering the promises of God and the posture of our hearts, we encounter a love that is greater than any heart-filled eyes or tender affection. God authored the love that informs and instructs any possible love that we could know with others. What kind of love sends His most beloved Son to walk dusty roads, to endure rejection, to suffer and die at the hands of those He seeks to love? What love breaks down every barrier to redeem His wandering, wayward creation? This love is the character of God, and this is the love that changes everything for a believer.

LOVE ISN'T A RESPONSE
WE MUSTER UP ON OUR OWN,
BUT RATHER, AN OUTWORKING
OF WHAT GROWS WITHIN US
WHEN WE FOLLOW IN HIS STEPS.

When Jesus gave His disciples the commandment to love—after they had walked with Him and witnessed the ways He loved people and God His Father—He made it clear that this command was rooted in imitation and implication. *Imitation* because they were called to love as He loved. *Implication* because to love as He loved meant that the onlooking world would know something of Christ-followers that their words alone could not infer. Francis Schaeffer put it this way: "Love—and the unity it attests to—is the mark Christ gave Christians to wear before the world. Only with this mark may the world know that Christians are indeed Christians and that Jesus was sent by the Father."[7]

Love isn't a response we muster up on our own, but rather, an outworking of what grows within us when we follow in His steps.

In this Advent season, let us take inventory. If the greatest commandment is to "love the Lord your God with all your heart and with all your soul and with all your mind...And a second is like it: You shall love your neighbor as yourself" (Matthew 22:36-40), then our source of any love toward neighbor, community, or country must come from an all-consuming love of God in our own hearts. What fills us up will inevitably overflow.

So, we look to Moses' words in Psalm 90:14 and borrow them as a prayer for ourselves: "Satisfy us in the morning with your steadfast love, that we may rejoice and be glad all our days."

Love

...LOVE ONE ANOTHER...

When the love of God, cradled in a lowly manger, becomes our greatest gift of the Christmas season and throughout the year, we can't help but lavish such love onto others...and declare His love with our actions before a watching world.

PONDER

As you consider God's extravagant love in your life, ask yourself: Who is He calling you to extend that love to this Christmas season?

PRAISE

Good Christian Men, Rejoice

PRAYER

Father, let nothing in this season and in this life satisfy so much as Your steadfast love. Show us the ways we have loved things or people more than we've found our satisfaction in You. Make us good students of Your love, that we might follow Your example and love out of the overflow of our hearts. And may You be glorified—by the way we love You, and by the way we love those You've placed in our lives.

SATISFY US
IN THE MORNING WITH
YOUR STEADFAST LOVE,
THAT WE MAY
REJOICE AND BE GLAD
ALL OUR DAYS.

Oh sing to the LORD a new song; sing to the LORD, all the earth! Sing to the LORD, bless his name; tell of his salvation from day to day. Declare his glory among the nations, his marvelous works among all the peoples! For great is the LORD, and greatly to be praised; he is to be feared above all gods.

Psalm 96:1-4

Day 18

Worship

John Piper famously said, "Missions exists because worship doesn't."[8] In other words, God desired relationship with us from the beginning. We were created to praise Him as our good and faithful God! When we tell the good news of Jesus' birth, life, death, and resurrection, we extend the invitation to return to God's desire for His people to worship Him—to love Him and be loved *by* Him as we read about yesterday; this is the ultimate goal of God's pursuit of His people.

While Jesus' birth served to relieve a hurting world, to bring hope to the hopeless, and to fulfill God's promise to reconcile His people to Himself, those who anticipated His birth responded first and foremost in worship.

All those who came to the manger came with bowed knees, humbled hearts, exuberant praise. Jesus, even in the form of an infant, was *God with us*, and in His presence, even the wise men knew their place. They brought gifts fit for a king because they knew He was worthy and worthy of treasuring.

How that first Christmas contrasts to our upside-down ideas of treasure and treasuring today. The simplicity and humble context of Christ's birth is wildly different than the extravagant display of *stuff* and self-gratification that marks much of modern-day Christmas celebrations in the West. While there's nothing inherently harmful about beautiful decorations, lavish gifts, holiday parties, or memories made with friends and family, so many miss the true worship they were made for when they settle for the worship of lesser things that don't really satisfy. Like the newest tech gadgets. Like Pinterest-worthy decor. Like family peace held together by a careful sidestepping of eggshells. Or getting the gift you really wanted or the affirmation you believe you deserve.

If you long for something that doesn't truly satisfy and only causes you to grasp more anxiously in striving for it, you're worshipping something other than Jesus.

COME TO THE MANGER AND
SURRENDER YOUR GREATEST TREASURES—
THEY DON'T EVEN COMPARE TO HIM.

You see, we can't truly encounter Christ the Messiah without the awe and wonder, the response of faith, the repentance, the thanksgiving, the love, and the worship He deserves. This week of our Advent journey is the heart's response to the promise of God through Christ, the Savior. If we find our response different than that of true worship, today is a good day to come to Jesus to give up that which we treasure most. If we're honest, that's ourselves. So come to Jesus, the King. Come to the manger and surrender your greatest treasures—they don't even compare to Him. Jesus is worthy of worship, and because of God's faithfulness through Christ, we are made worthy *to worship* Him. Joy to the world!

Worship

WORSHIP THE LORD IN THE
SPLENDOR OF HOLINESS...

PONDER

Who (or what) are you truly worshipping during this Advent season?
If it's not Jesus, ask Him to realign your heart to worship Him alone.

PRAISE

Angels, from the Realms of Glory

PRAY

God, You are great and greatly to be praised.
Draw our hearts back to You when we're tempted
to give our praise and adoration to lesser things.
You alone are worthy of our worship! Amen.

GOD'S GREATEST DELIGHT
IS YOUR DELIGHT IN HIM.

SAM STORMS

[Simeon] came in the Spirit into the temple, and when the parents brought in the child Jesus, to do for him according to the custom of the Law, he took him up in his arms and blessed God and said, "Lord, now you are letting your servant depart in peace, according to your word; for my eyes have seen your salvation that you have prepared in the presence of all peoples, a light for revelation to the Gentiles, and for glory to your people Israel."

Luke 2:27-32

WEEK FOUR

Our Messiah

WEEK FOUR

Our Messiah

The word *Messiah* literally means "anointed one," and is synonymous with *Christ* (which wasn't Jesus' last name—*wink*—but a title). Jesus was no ordinary man. He was the God-man, sent by the Father to bring salvation to all who put their trust in Him. This long-awaited arrival of the anointed one was the reason for Simeon's rejoicing—an echo of creation's groaning for a Savior.

And in the same way Jesus came seeking repentance and surrender, He still invites us now, 2,000 years later, to prepare Him room. Jesus could've come in grandeur, demanding reverence and allegiance, but He didn't. Instead, our Messiah chose to define real salvation and deliverance—an eternal kind of rescue. Jesus taught people to re-posture their hearts. He demonstrated how He fulfilled God's promise, and how we—His children—are made to respond. This is the very journey we've been on together this Christmas season. It's all about Jesus.

Let's finish out this final week by remembering exactly who this Messiah truly is and why we can trust Him—now and throughout the year.

To us a child is born,
   to us a son is given;
and the government shall be upon his shoulder,
   and his name shall be called
Wonderful Counselor, Mighty God,
   Everlasting Father, Prince of Peace.
Of the increase of his government and of peace
   there will be no end,
on the throne of David and over his kingdom,
   to establish it and to uphold it
with justice and with righteousness
   from this time forth and forevermore.
The zeal of the LORD of hosts will do this.

Isaiah 9:6-7

Day 19

Wonderful Counselor

I f only the cares of this life took a holiday during the Christmas season. If only the questions, health diagnoses, unknowns, fears, and not-yet-resolved issues all magically uncomplicated themselves while we seek to celebrate and savor Advent. But chances are you've acquired a collection of concerns and questions as plentiful as the ornaments that come out year after year. Unlike treasured Christmas decor, this collection overstays its welcome and feels burdensome when its contents linger and surface again and again.

You may be in such a season. Maybe you've been waking up each day, thinking, *If only someone could just tell me what to do.* Perhaps you're a high school graduate trying to decide which college to commit to. Maybe you're a mom struggling to know the words to speak to a hurting child. Maybe you're a teen wrestling with choices no one knows about. Perhaps this season finds you asking big questions about life, purpose, meaning, and where to find hope.

For all of us lacking wisdom or struggling with the unknowns we are walking through in this season, Jesus is our Wonderful Counselor. *Wonderful*

Counselor is one of Jesus' names. Giving counsel is what He does. He is our true source of hope and help, directing us to His good purposes and His right ways. Jesus, our Counselor, is the only one who can truly satisfy the questions and wrestlings of our hearts because He's the one who knows every detail about us and the plans He has for us.

> BECAUSE JESUS BECAME FLESH AND DWELT AMONG US, HE CAN SAY FROM EXPERIENCE, "I UNDERSTAND WHAT YOU ARE GOING THROUGH."

Literally translated "a wonder of a counselor," the name *Wonderful Counselor* reminds us that our Savior is all-wise, all-knowing, all-loving, all-powerful. He holds wisdom that we can't even fathom! Do you remember Job's conversation with God? Do you remember what David wrote in Psalm 139? "Such knowledge is too wonderful for me; it is high; I cannot attain it" (verse 6). What overwhelms us does not overwhelm Jesus.

Because Jesus became flesh and dwelt among us, He can say from experience, "I understand what you are going through." And because He is God, He possesses perfect wisdom that is backed by perfect love. Fully human and fully divine, there is no greater counselor we could ask for!

With Jesus, our access to counsel is unlimited. We can ask for it in prayer (James 1:5). The Spirit indwells us, ever ready to guide us (John 14:26). And we have God's perfect Word, that we "may be complete" (2 Timothy 3:17). So call upon Him—your Wonderful Counselor!

Wonderful Counselor

...HIS NAME SHALL BE
CALLED WONDERFUL
COUNSELOR...

He is all-wise

With Jesus to counsel our hearts, we are never lacking. The hope and assurance He gives is within our reach at all times. We are never without help.

PONDER

What lack of understanding do you need to take
to your Wonderful Counselor today?

PRAISE

For Unto Us a Child Is Born

PRAY

Wonderful Counselor, thank You for Your nearness.
We're leaning in to listen. We want Your ways, Your heart,
Your plans instead of our own. Help us to find Your counsel
truly wonderful and more than we could imagine. Amen.

SUCH KNOWLEDGE IS
TOO WONDERFUL FOR ME;
IT IS HIGH; I CANNOT
ATTAIN IT.

PSALM *139:6*

The LORD your God is in your midst,
  a mighty one who will save;
he will rejoice over you with gladness;
  he will quiet you by his love;
he will exult over you with loud singing.

Zephaniah 3:17

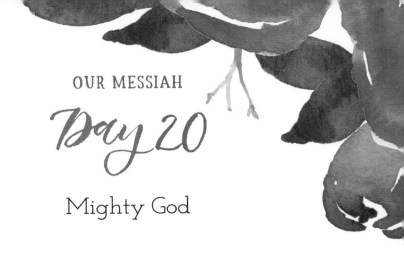

Day 20

Mighty God

Do you find it surprising that the God of the universe came to earth in the form of a baby? He didn't choose the decadence of a royal palace. He didn't arrive on the back of a shooting star—though He could have. The God who spoke this world into existence and controls the very waves of the sea didn't show His strength and might through displays of power. A fireworks show? A global telecast? A fleet of chartered ships? A royal red carpet? A banquet for thousands? God could've commanded anything He desired to usher His beloved Son, Jesus, into the world. Instead of grandeur, God chose to display His might through humility and wonder in the ordinary.

We're often tempted to expect God to display His power through miraculous signs and dramatic acts of might. (Be honest: Don't we sometimes expect God to be like Santa Claus, delivering all the good to the deserving and somehow "getting the memo" on all our wishes and longings?) But our Messiah is no Santa Claus. He doesn't simply promise to deliver gifts; He promises to be the gift we truly need.

How has He provided for you in mighty ways during this season? How has the good news of Jesus been the gift your soul needs? Consider the meals you don't have to wonder about. Think about the ways He's carried you through trials and difficult times. Remember how God has faithfully allowed you to conquer some of the impossible circumstances in your life. Is He mighty to save? Yes, yes, He is.

When we count the ways He has been mighty in loving, consistent, and ordinary ways, we start to understand what Zephaniah meant when he wrote that the "mighty one who will save" shows His power by covering us with His love and delight. Of all the ways God can show His might and power, He chooses to sing over us, rejoice over us, quiet and comfort us. That ought to stop us in our tracks. While we covet dramatic solutions and pine after miraculous wonders, God wants us to be overcome with His mighty love.

JESUS THE MESSIAH DIDN'T COME MERELY TO FIX YOUR PROBLEMS BUT TO FILL YOUR HEART.

Just as the Israelites had hoped to be saved by a political savior or a conquering warrior, we so often miss the true gift of Jesus, our Messiah. We settle for so much less than the mighty love of Jesus, the mighty faithfulness of Jesus, the mighty rescue of Jesus. When we discover God's might and His love in unison, we finally begin to understand how we can be "quieted by His love."

Mighty God

...A MIGHTY ONE WHO
WILL SAVE...

Do you feel chaotic in your mind or heart in this season, looking for solutions to your overwhelming concerns? Jesus the Messiah didn't come merely to fix your problems but to fill your heart. He is mighty to save what could be otherwise lost to the ruin of sin and self-centeredness. You have hope under the covering of almighty God.

PONDER

How does Zephaniah 3:17 change the way you think about your current struggles and concerns?

PRAISE

Infant Holy, Infant Lowly

PRAY

Almighty God, we thank You for being so much greater, so much stronger, so much more powerful than our greatest needs and our worst fears. Thank You for quieting us with Your love and for the constant reminder through Your Word that we are both safe and secure in Your care. Amen.

YOU WILL NEVER NEED
MORE THAN GOD
CAN SUPPLY.

J.I. PACKER

I saw in the night visions,

and behold, with the clouds of heaven
there came one like a son of man,
and he came to the Ancient of Days
and was presented before him.
And to him was given dominion
and glory and a kingdom,
that all peoples, nations, and languages
should serve him;
his dominion is an everlasting dominion,
which shall not pass away,
and his kingdom one
that shall not be destroyed.

Daniel 7:13-14

Day 21

Everlasting Father

In just a few short weeks, people all over the world will put away their nativity sets and the sights and sounds of Christmas will fade for another year. (Which is your home: Team Take Down by New Years,' or Team Wait Until February?) Regardless of how long we linger or how long we wear our Christmas pajamas, eventually we put away the ornaments and take down the twinkle lights, and our homes are hushed in the wake of a new season.

No good thing lasts forever. Except God.

It may be hard for us to wrap our minds around eternal things in a world where the prettiest bouquets fade and die, where relationships end, or where we say goodbye to those we love. And when Scripture calls Christ, our Messiah, the Everlasting Father, we might feel doubly unsure when earthly fathers fall short of always keeping their promises, always being there for us.

"I and the Father are one," Jesus says in John 10:30. What sounded blasphemous to His unbelieving Jewish listeners is utter comfort and assurance to us who trust Jesus as our Savior. Because God the Father is eternal, all-powerful, all-knowing, patient, merciful, trustworthy, sovereign, and good, so is Jesus. God's ways are never-ending. And the best news of all? He made sure we would know the very presence of His Everlasting Father-ness by sending His Son, Jesus, to walk among us, and then the Holy Spirit to dwell in us. Everlasting can feel far away and beyond imagination until you discover that the good news of Jesus is that because of Him, we are brought near to God's eternal love and welcome.

EXPERIENCING ACCESS TO OUR EVERLASTING FATHER CAN BEGIN RIGHT NOW SIMPLY BY PUTTING OUR TRUST IN HIM.

Even Jesus' prayer to His Father defines the eternal in an immediate way on our behalf:

> This is eternal life, that they know you, the only true God, and Jesus Christ whom you have sent (John 17:3).

Do you know what this means? It means we don't need to wait for heaven to know the joy of eternal life. The eternal, unending, everlasting life-giving hope of salvation through Jesus starts now when we taste and see that the Lord is good. Experiencing access to our Everlasting Father can begin right now simply by putting our trust in Him. Paul David Tripp says it this way:

> By his life, death, and resurrection, Jesus welcomes us into his family. He is the door by which we have access to God. He lavishes his fatherly love upon us, and we are blessed with all the

Everlasting Father

...HIS DOMINION IS AN
EVERLASTING DOMINION...

He never changes

rights and privileges of being his children. No longer separated, lost, alienated, and alone, we live forever as the sons and daughters of the King.[9]

God is our perfect Father, and His faithfulness never ends. His presence is made available to us the moment we turn from trusting in ourselves to trusting in Jesus for sin's remedy.

When you are tempted to feel alone in this Christmas season, remember that Jesus left His Father's side to make a way for us to be adopted as sons and daughters into His Father's kingdom. In Christ we have an Everlasting Father—we are never alone!

PONDER
How is God a good Father to you?

PRAISE
While Shepherds Watched Their Flocks

PRAY
Everlasting Father, You have been faithful from the beginning of time and You will be faithful to the end. Thank You for making a way for us to join You in everlasting fellowship with the Son and the Spirit. We can't know Your presence apart from the work of Christ on the cross, so we place our trust in Him as we long to know You more. Amen.

HIS DOMINION IS AN
EVERLASTING DOMINION,
WHICH SHALL NOT PASS AWAY.

DANIEL 7:14

He shall stand and shepherd his flock in the
    strength of the LORD,
      in the majesty of the name of the LORD his God.
And they shall dwell secure, for now he shall be great
    to the ends of the earth.
And he shall be their peace.

Micah 5:4-5

Day 22

Prince of Peace

If we're honest, some of us aren't wishing for things like scooters, new clothes, or tech gadgets this Christmas; some of us have Christmas lists with longings more like these:

- ☐ Mom and Dad getting along
- ☐ A best friend
- ☐ A broken heart mended
- ☐ Reconciliation of a broken relationship
- ☐ Peace in our nation
- ☐ Getting out of debt
- ☐ To be cancer-free
- ☐ End to all the bickering at home

In other words, we long for peace: between siblings, with parents, among friends, on social media, and within our own chaotic hearts.

Today, peace seems as elusive as ever, with political unrest, injustice, economic unknowns, and unprecedented levels of loneliness and anxiety in a digitally connected world. The ancient world may not have had the same stressors that plague the modern age, but people sought to know peace just the same. They too believed that peace would come in the form of worldly justice, comfort, or political victory. But Jesus offered a peace much greater than their circumstances:

> Peace I leave with you; my peace I give to you. Not as the world gives do I give to you. Let not your hearts be troubled, neither let them be afraid (John 14:27).

Jesus is called the Prince of Peace because apart from His sacrifice on the cross, we would still, in our sin, be enemies of a holy God. Where there is sin, there is no peace. Think about the last time you were at odds with someone—what sin was at play that resulted in your lack of peace? Was it pride? Anger? Selfishness? Trace the conflict—the lack of peace—back to its source. Inevitably, the absence of peace with others or even within yourself begins with sin and a lack of trust in God.

The cross of Christ was the bridge God provided to lead us back to peace with Him. Jesus removed the separation from God that our rebellion caused and made it possible for us to be restored to our Creator on account of His perfect righteousness. We access the peace of God when we surrender to the Prince of Peace. When we give Jesus, the Prince of Peace, His rightful place on the throne of our hearts, He brings peace to every area of our lives—our thoughts, our relationships, our daily labors, our trials. It's not a magic pill; it's a message that transforms. The more we are filled with the truth of God's provision, the more we learn to desire the peace of God rather than the peace the world offers.

THE PEACE WE EXPERIENCE IN OUR EVERYDAY LIVES BECOMES AN OVERFLOW OF THE PEACE WE KNOW WHEN THE PRINCE OF PEACE RULES OUR HEARTS.

Prince of Peace

...HE SHALL BE
THEIR PEACE.

He is our peace

Only in Christ—the Prince of Peace—can we know the peace that replaces disagreement with unity, turmoil with calm, strife with harmony, restlessness with contentment, angst with joy. The peace we experience in our everyday lives becomes an overflow of the peace we know when the Prince of Peace rules our hearts.

We long for peace, and sometimes at Christmas, we think we can find it through candlelit rooms, gatherings of loved ones, and neighborly acts of kindness. But don't settle for the kind of peace temporary things offer. While the season is filled with beautiful ways to express peace, even lovely attempts at creating a peaceful atmosphere fall short of giving us true peace. The Prince of Peace offers, instead, everlasting rest in Him. Jesus alone is the author of peace; His life, death, and resurrection have purchased the enduring rest our souls desire. That Christmas list with wishes for peace? It's met in Jesus, even now.

PONDER
Where do you look to find peace? Does it satisfy?

PRAISE
Hark! the Herald Angels Sing

PRAY
Prince of Peace, thank You for being the calm, the comfort, the rest, and the unshakable peace we can't secure on our own. In this season, teach us to be satisfied with nothing less than peace with You and peace in You. Amen.

WHAT PEACE CAN THEY
HAVE WHO ARE NOT AT
PEACE WITH GOD?

MATTHEW HENRY

I saw heaven opened, and behold, a white horse! The one sitting on it is called Faithful and True, and in righteousness he judges and makes war. His eyes are like a flame of fire, and on his head are many diadems, and he has a name written that no one knows but himself. He is clothed in a robe dipped in blood, and the name by which he is called is The Word of God. And the armies of heaven, arrayed in fine linen, white and pure, were following him on white horses. From his mouth comes a sharp sword with which to strike down the nations, and he will rule them with a rod of iron. He will tread the winepress of the fury of the wrath of God the Almighty. On his robe and on his thigh he has a name written, King of kings and Lord of lords.

Revelation 19:11-16

Day 23

Lord of Lords

When the angel announced the Savior's birth to the shepherds, he identified this newborn by His heavenly title "Christ the Lord" (Luke 2:11). Though He was born in a stable and wore no crown, the angel made it clear who Jesus was. To call Jesus Lord is to call Him God.

We tend to think a lot about Christ as Savior and to thank Him for the gift of salvation, but do we think enough about Christ as Lord and thank Him for His sovereignty? The title *Lord* signifies rule and reign, authority and commander-in-chief. In other words, Jesus is Lord because Jesus is the boss—the one who has the final say on everything in our lives.

So often, we are enamored with the Jesus who can rescue us from eternal separation from God, but we chafe at the lordship of Jesus. To be brought near to God is to belong to Him. Spurgeon said it poignantly this way: "If Christ is not all to you, He is nothing to you; He will never go into partnership as a part Saviour of men. If He is something, He must be everything, and if He be not everything, He is nothing to you."[10]

Whoever or whatever sits on the throne of your heart is who or what rules your life. A king's power is absolute. When we fail to submit to Christ in some way or other, we have made His rule over us less than absolute, and we are treating Him as less than King. Allegiance to the lordship of Christ isn't like joining the military. We don't sign a contract or promise to uphold a set of rules lest we be penalized. Submitting to the lordship of Christ in our lives should be a joyful laying down of our own wills in recognition that our King, Jesus, is stronger, better, more loving, and more satisfying than anything else we could align our lives with.

Do we profess Him as our King? Then we should commit ourselves to live accordingly.

WHAT A DELIGHT LIFE BECOMES
WHEN WE MAKE CHRIST MASTER
OVER EVERYTHING!

The book of Revelation describes Jesus' second coming as King, as Lord of All. The whole earth will one day give Jesus, the Messiah, the honor He is due, whether they chose to submit to His rule or not. But we who believe and trust in Jesus shouldn't wait for that day. We are to trust Him to rule our lives now. What a delight life becomes when we make Christ master over everything! And how miserable life becomes when we cling to a throne that is not rightfully ours.

This Christmas, don't miss the joy and peace that comes when you surrender the throne of your heart to the Lord of lords, Jesus, and recognize that He alone is deserving—"that at the name of Jesus every knee should bow,

Lord of Lords

...HE HAS A NAME WRITTEN,
KING OF KINGS AND
LORD OF LORDS.

He is Lord of all

in heaven and on earth and under the earth, and every tongue confess that Jesus Christ is Lord, to the glory of God the Father" (Philippians 2:10-11).

The search is over: Only Jesus is worthy of being King of kings and Lord of lords. When Jesus is more than a friend, more than a helper, more than a shoulder to lean on—when He is the Master of your life—you experience Christmas in a different way. He isn't just the long-awaited Messiah; He is what your heart has been longing for all along.

PONDER

What hinders your acknowledgment of Christ's lordship? What competes for your allegiance?

PRAISE

Angels We Have Heard on High

PRAY

Lord of lords, we confess the foolishness of trying to be the rulers of our own lives. We're sorry for attempting to take the place that belongs to You. Thank You for being trustworthy in every way; may we delight in being under Your care and Your will as we respond and declare, "Yes, Lord." Amen.

JESUS' KINGSHIP IS NOT
SOMETHING THAT REMAINS
IN THE FUTURE.
CHRIST IS KING
RIGHT THIS MINUTE.

R.C. SPROUL

Now the birth of Jesus Christ took place in this way. When his mother Mary had been betrothed to Joseph, before they came together she was found to be with child from the Holy Spirit. And her husband Joseph, being a just man and unwilling to put her to shame, resolved to divorce her quietly. But as he considered these things, behold, an angel of the Lord appeared to him in a dream, saying, "Joseph, son of David, do not fear to take Mary as your wife, for that which is conceived in her is from the Holy Spirit. She will bear a son, and you shall call his name Jesus, for he will save his people from their sins." All this took place to fulfill what the Lord had spoken by the prophet:

"Behold, the virgin shall conceive and bear a son,
and they shall call his name Immanuel"
(which means, God with us).

Matthew 1:18-23

Day 24

Immanuel

I f there's one name for Jesus that captures the whole heart of God, it is this: Immanuel—God with us. No other name so adequately expresses the fullness of God's desire from the beginning of time: to be in fellowship with His image-bearers and to be their God. He's always wanted us to be with Him. When sin broke that fellowship, God set into motion His plan to bring us back to Him. When we could not be with Him, He came to be with us.

Chances are this Christmas finds you feeling more alone in your personal struggles and thoughts than the busyness and festivities of this season might suggest. Maybe it's physical distance from those you love, or maybe it's emotional. And maybe the challenges of this year have you wondering if you're the only one who struggles like you do. Our enemy, Satan, just as he did in the Garden, would love for us to think God has abandoned us—that He has left us to fend for ourselves.

Most of us experienced the effects of isolation and distancing that a global pandemic brought. And those effects were compounded for an already-lonely generation. The separation we felt during that global crisis was not unlike the separation that sin causes in our lives. It isolates, it hides, it removes us from the comfort of others. Sin robs us of the very nearness we were created to have with our Creator, God. The weary world that looked for their Messiah couldn't fix the problem of pain and brokenness that sin set loose. They needed God to do the impossible, and He did.

The name *Immanuel* emphasizes God's nearness to us when we were unable to be near to Him. For us as believers, God is with us; He is not without us or against us. This truth reveals the heart of God. It makes His promise in Matthew 28:20, "I am with you always," all the more special. We are never alone.

GOD WITH US IS THE
TRUE GIFT OF CHRISTMAS.

This is the good news: That God with us (Matthew 1:23)—the Lord Jesus Christ—left His Father's side to be with us, live among us, and to be crucified so that He could become God in us (Colossians 1:27) and God for us (Romans 8:31-32). Without God with us, we would not celebrate Christmas. Without Christmas, we would not celebrate the resurrection. Without the resurrection, we would not have the hope of eternity with God. Redemption—God's rescue of us from our sin—has always been about being with our God, our Father, forever—unhindered, unashamed, unafraid, undone by the greatness and great love of God.

God with us is the true gift of Christmas. For all the human effort and our insufficient means of paving a way back to fellowship with Him, God closes the gap and makes the only way through His Son. He came to us!

Immanuel

...THEY SHALL CALL HIS
NAME IMMANUEL...

He is
God
with
us

The weary world rejoices, indeed. And in our rejoicing, we relax our shoulders, sigh in great relief, and sing, "O come to us, abide with us, our Lord Immanuel!"

PONDER
How does God's pursuit of you change your heart for Him?

PRAISE
O Holy Night!

PRAY
Immanuel, You are the reason we celebrate. You came to us when we could not get ourselves back to You. This is amazing grace. Thank You, Jesus. Because of You, we are never alone. May we never cease to rejoice over what You have done for us! Amen.

O COME TO US,
ABIDE WITH US,
OUR LORD
IMMANUEL.

PHILLIPS BROOKS

Christmas Day

...THE LORD IS COME.

Day 25

Christmas Day

Today is a day of rejoicing. If we've prepared Him room in our hearts, believed His promises, responded in faith, and considered the Messiah we celebrate, then today is more than the birthday of Jesus; it is the day we remember where our lasting joy comes from. And when our joy is eternal, today—Christmas Day—isn't the end of our celebrations; it is but the beginning. This joy is meant to change us 365 days of the year. And when we forget that, we simply need to remember this truth:

> God so loved the world, that he gave his only Son, that whoever believes in him should not perish but have eternal life (John 3:16).

It's a Christmas gift so amazing and true we can't help but continue—day after day, year after year—to prepare Him room, now and always.

Let us take time together to celebrate the miracle of God with us by reading the Christmas story as given in the Gospel of Luke.

The Christmas Story

LUKE 2:1-20

In those days a decree went out from Caesar Augustus that all the world should be registered. This was the first registration when Quirinius was governor of Syria. And all went to be registered, each to his own town. And Joseph also went up from Galilee, from the town of Nazareth, to Judea, to the city of David, which is called Bethlehem, because he was of the house and lineage of David, to be registered with Mary, his betrothed, who was with child. And while they were there, the time came for her to give birth. And she gave birth to her firstborn son and wrapped him in swaddling cloths and laid him in a manger, because there was no place for them in the inn.

And in the same region there were shepherds out in the field, keeping watch over their flock by night. And an angel of the Lord appeared to them, and the glory of the Lord shone around them, and they were filled with great fear. And the angel said to them, "Fear not, for behold, I bring you good news of great joy that will be for all the people. For unto you is born this day in the city of David a Savior, who is Christ the Lord. And this will be a sign for you: you will find a baby wrapped in swaddling cloths and lying in a manger." And suddenly there was with the angel a multitude of the heavenly host praising God and saying,

> "Glory to God in the highest,
>> And on earth peace among those
>> with whom he is pleased!"

When the angels went away from them into heaven, the shepherds said to one another, "Let us go over to Bethlehem and see this thing that has happened, which the Lord has made known to us." And they went with haste and found Mary and Joseph, and the baby lying in a manger. And when they saw it, they made known the saying that had been told them concerning this child. And all who heard it wondered at what the shepherds told them. But Mary treasured up all these things, pondering them in her heart. And the shepherds returned, glorifying and praising God for all they had heard and seen, as it had been told them.

FOR UNTO YOU
IS BORN THIS DAY
IN THE CITY OF
DAVID A SAVIOR,
WHO IS CHRIST
THE LORD.

Notes

1. Corrie ten Boom, *In My Father's House* (Eureka, MT: Lighthouse Trails Publishing, 2011), 146.

2. A.W. Tozer, "No Looking Back," *The Alliance Tozer Devotional*, Friday, November 6, 2020, www.cmalliance.org/devotions/tozer?id=518.

3. Elyse Fitzpatrick, "I Just Don't Understand!," *Elyse Fitzpatrick*, www.elysefitzpatrick.com/i-just-dont-understand/.

4. Paul M. Gould and Daniel Ray, gen. eds., *The Story of the Cosmos* (Eugene, OR: Harvest House Publishers, 2019), 9.

5. A significant portion of this paragraph appears in the foreword I wrote for Elisa Pulliam's book *Unblinded Faith* (Eugene, OR: Harvest House, 2018), 9.

6. The first three lines of this paragraph appear in the foreword I wrote for Elisa Pulliam's book *Unblinded Faith*, 9-10.

7. Francis Schaeffer, *The Mark of the Christian* (Downers Grove, IL: InterVarsity Press, 1976), 35.

8. John Piper, "Missions Exists Because Worship Doesn't," *Desiring God*, www.desiring god.org/messages/missions-exists-because-worship-doesnt-a-bethlehem-legacy-inherited-and-bequeathed.

9. Paul David Tripp, "My Favorite Christmas Bible Verse," *PT*, December 11, 2019, www.paul tripp.com/wednesdays-word/posts/my-favorite-christmas-bible-verse.

10. C.H. Spurgeon, "Christ Is All," sermon preached at the Metropolitan Tabernacle on August 20, 1871.

Acknowledgments

This book had its beginning during a phone call several years ago between me and my GraceLaced Shoppe product developer, Gina Adams. We were brainstorming ways to bless the GraceLaced.com community with artwork that could point to the simple truths of the gospel at Christmastime. We called the 25-day card set *Prepare Him Room*. I wanted the cards to feel like our family devotional, *Foundations*, which can be read aloud and shared with family and friends. I shared the vision, Gina worked through my outline, and Sarah Alexander, my designer at GraceLaced, transformed my artwork into beautiful pieces of art that went onto the cards, which were created to be used during the Advent season. So I first want to thank my creative and editorial team at GraceLaced, the unsung heroes of the work I get to share with our community online.

We knew there was so much more from God's Word to be unearthed than could fit onto small cards for reflection, so a book was born.

THANK YOU...

to my team at Harvest House Publishers for catching the vision, the passion, and the desire I had to create an unconventional Advent journey. Thank you for believing in the way God has wired me and my creativity. Thank you for supporting my message and giving it wings to fly.

to Janelle Coury for creating a beautiful experience in book form once again, and to Ruth Samsel, for lending your eye for creativity and detail.

to my editor and friend, Steve Miller: I get teary when I think of the immense support, care, and dedication you gave to this project. You fueled my writing with more than research and suggestions; you helped me to worship as I worked. These words are an overflow of the hours you poured into my personal growth, encouragement, and making sure I was equipped as an author. Thank you being a shepherd kind of editor.

to my agent, Jenni Burke—your creative support and encouragement was so timely.

to Eve Stipes, my friend and co-laborer in ministry: I'm grateful for your thoughtful input that brings excellence and clarity to each of my projects. Thanks for caring for my words as if they were your own.

And to Troy and the boys...
thank you for the endless conversations around the dinner table and in the car that overflowed into the words on these pages. You help me to know Jesus as Emmanuel, God with us, every day of the year.

Finally, thank you to the One who never leaves us nor forsakes us—Jesus, our Emmanuel. You are worthy of our adoration and praise, always.

About the Author

RUTH CHOU SIMONS is a *Wall Street Journal* bestselling and award-winning author of several books, including *GraceLaced*, *Beholding and Becoming*, and *Foundations*. She is an artist, entrepreneur, and speaker, using each of these platforms to spiritually sow the Word of God into people's hearts. Through her online shoppe at GraceLaced.com and her social media community, Simons shares her journey of God's grace intersecting daily life with word and art. Ruth and her husband, Troy, are grateful parents to six boys—their greatest adventure.

Wrapped in Yuletide Cheer

RUTH CHOU SIMONS

FOUNDER OF *gracelaced*

Christmas
Gift Wrap

12 PATTERNED SHEETS

Add extra beauty to your Christmas gifts with lovely holiday artwork from Ruth Chou Simons! These vibrant prints are perfect for wrapping a thoughtful present, sprucing up an empty wall, adding to your next art project, or turning into a backdrop for that perfect Instagram photo. Each sheet features a different seasonal design and comes with its own matching gift tag.

Read the Beloved Books of Ruth Chou Simons